"I called Chip Merlin to help with over twenty of my municipal clients with insurance issues from Superstorm Sandy. I got to see firsthand why they call him the 'Babe Ruth of hurricane attorneys.' When it comes to insurance claims, Chip Merlin is the person all others should listen to and learn from."

—Lawrence E. Bathgate, II
Senior partner, Bathgate, Wegener & Wolf, P.C.

"Chip Merlin has been a respected industry thought leader for over thirty-five years. I often seek his counsel on property insurance disputes and am confident that the wisdom he imparts in this book will provide great insight and value to consumers."

—Paul Handerhan
Former president, Florida Association of Public Insurance Adjusters

"If anyone knows how to get an insurer to pay up, it's Chip Merlin, a true policyholder advocate with an unmatched track record of righting insurance wrongs and helping people collect what they are owed."

—Amy Bach
Executive director, United Policyholders

"Chip dedicates his time and energy to informing both policyholders and adjusters on how to best navigate bad faith insurers through his practice and speaking engagements across the country. When you want the best, you call Chip Merlin. This book condenses all that knowledge into one go-to source that should be read by anyone with any type of property insurance."

—Lisa A. Kline, Esq.
Corporate general counsel

"As one of the nation's leading advocates for insurance consumers, Chip Merlin knows how to get insurance companies to honor the promise of security they make in their insurance policies."

—Jay Feinman
Professor of insurance law, Rutgers University; author, Delay, Deny, Defend: Why Insurance Companies Don't Pay Claims and What You Can Do about It

"Chip is the master of explaining the importance of ethical behavior by all parties within the claims process to policyholders. His thirty-plus years of experience in the field provide a wealth of information that every policyholder should seek out. He uses this as a tool to enable the insurance company to pay what they owe. Woe to them if they don't!"

—Scott DeLuise
Former president, National Association of Public Insurance Adjusters

"Chip Merlin is a passionate advocate for policyholder rights. His widely read blog is relied upon as a leading national authority for guidance in claims handling and insurance trends. Whenever Chip is writing something about insurance, it should be read by all stakeholders in the insurance industry!"

—Holly Soffer
General counsel, America Association of Public Insurance Adjusters

"If I had an insurance claim dispute that I was unable to resolve with the insurance company, the first person I would seek counsel from would be Chip Merlin. In my fifty years working in the insurance industry, I have not encountered a more competent and professional policyholder attorney."

—Bill Wilson, CPCU, ARM
Author, When Worlds Collide: Resolving Insurance Coverage and Claims Disputes

CHIP MERLIN

PAY UP!

PREVENTING A DISASTER
WITH YOUR OWN INSURANCE COMPANY

ForbesBooks

Published by ForbesBooks, Charleston, South Carolina.
Member of Advantage Media Group.

ForbesBooks is a registered trademark, and the ForbesBooks colophon is a trademark of Forbes Media, LLC.

Printed in the United States of America.

10 9 8 7 6 5 4 3 2 1

ISBN: 978-1-94663-382-8
LCCN: 2019920097

Book design by Wesley Strickland.

This publication is designed to provide accurate and authoritative information in regard to the subject matter covered. It is sold with the understanding that the publisher is not engaged in rendering legal, accounting, or other professional services. If legal advice or other expert assistance is required, the services of a competent professional person should be sought.

Advantage Media Group is proud to be a part of the Tree Neutral® program. Tree Neutral offsets the number of trees consumed in the production and printing of this book by taking proactive steps such as planting trees in direct proportion to the number of trees used to print books. To learn more about Tree Neutral, please visit **www.treeneutral.com.**

Since 1917, the Forbes mission has remained constant. Global Champions of Entrepreneurial Capitalism. ForbesBooks exists to further that aim by bringing the Stories, Passion, and Knowledge of top thought leaders to the forefront. ForbesBooks brings you The Best in Business. To be considered for publication, please visit **www.forbesbooks.com.**

ACKNOWLEDGMENTS

I have a village of people to thank, who have taught me lessons shared in this book, who encouraged me to write about my experiences, and who made this possible. Inherently, some are missed because there are so many that have blessed me in my career representing policyholders and learning my trade.

The law is a very jealous mistress and takes time from family and close friends. My children Chase and Austin are the best any father could hope for. Bill Merlin, Alice Merlin, Kim Merlin, Emily Merlin, and Mary Alice Merlin Floyd have always provided encouragement. Donice Krueger has been my support and offered numerous suggestions.

Merlin Law Group attorneys and staff have also played an important part of this book, especially Keona Williams, Mary Fortson, Eunice Elias, Shane Smith, and Robin Bradley.

I am indebted to all public adjusters. Mentioning long-ago experiences with Harvey Goodman, Dick Tutwiler, Karl Denison, the late Ira Sarasohn, Randy Goodman, Ron Papa, and Ray Altieri just scratches the surface in doing justice to the hundreds of great public adjusters helping people every day. Public adjuster Don Wood and his family helped encourage me to finish this book.

Wise mentors and leaders in the insurance field willing to spend time collaborating with me have been a blessing as well. Amy Bach, Gary Fye, Charles Miller, Bill Wilson, and the late Eugene Anderson have played significant roles in shaping my understanding of insurance from the policyholder's perspective. Ruck DeMinico and Kim Dvorak have acted as researchers, finding the exact information I have needed.

The ForbesBooks team has been a blessing and a joy to work with. My close collaboration with Andrew Mortazavi truly made this book. Rachel Griffin kept me moving on schedule, and the book would not have been completed without her.

CONTENTS

HOW I BECAME AN ATTORNEY FOR POLICYHOLDERS

WHEN I WAS ONLY about ten years old, the water heater in our house broke down. I'll never forget overhearing my mother saying to my father, "If anything else breaks, we won't have the money to fix it." My father was a lieutenant commander in the United States Coast Guard. My mother was a nurse. My parents were frugal, but like a lot of middle-class families, we still lived paycheck to paycheck.

My mom's words taught me two things that shaped my life. First, I didn't want to join the military. The military did not pay its officers much money during the Vietnam War. While I have total respect and admiration for those who serve, I am not the kind of person who could take orders to move all over the world without having much say in the decision. Second, I wanted a job that would pay enough money to afford simple repairs without breaking the bank.

However, I was not certain what path to take in life. All I knew was that I was going to the University of Florida. My father moved us around a lot for the military, but he held on to his Florida residency so that I could get less expensive in-state tuition. My plan was to get an undergraduate degree and then probably a graduate degree in business. But a month before starting college, my friend invited me on a family fishing trip to the Chesapeake Bay. His father picked me up in a station wagon on a Saturday afternoon after closing his dry cleaning shop. We made it about two miles down the road before an old man ran a stop sign. We crashed into his car and were sent over the median and head-on into a Volkswagen Bus.

It was a horrible accident. The people in the Volkswagen Bus were rushed to the hospital. My elbow and thumb were fractured, but since it wasn't life threatening, I asked the first responders to take me to the army hospital in Fort Belvoir. There weren't any orthopedic doctors at the military hospital when I arrived. The orthopedic doctor was out playing golf. Later, the medical staff helped straighten out the bone the best they could. To this day, I still can't straighten my arm.

My dad suggested that we not hire an attorney to deal with the fallout of the accident. In the 1940s his own father had a bad experience with lawyers that resulted in the family construction business losing a case they felt they should have won. The possibility of my becoming a lawyer was not a topic of discussion in our house. I had never even considered it. But the accident left me feeling powerless. I didn't know my rights or where I stood. Later, I saw that my friend and his family had their attorney involved in the matter. Everybody who was in the accident had a lawyer except me. It dawned on me that lawyers knew where they stood in the world because they knew the law. They knew their rights. They knew how to fight for those rights. They knew how to stand up for themselves and others.

Today I am more than three decades into a legal career. I couldn't be more satisfied with my decision to go into law. I still believe that knowing the law means knowing your rights. I also know my clients' rights—and I can fight for them. Every day for over thirty-five years now, my work has allowed me to be someone's champion. As an insurance claims attorney and policyholder advocate, I get to fight for the little guy, the underdog, the everyday people and business owners trying to make their way in the world and collect what they are owed by insurance companies. Sometimes it's not even about the money. Having a legitimate claim denied feels like a violation to most people. Policyholders feel vindicated when the insurance company finally acknowledges that they were right and their claim was just.

I may not be in the military, but my practice allows me the honor to fight for and serve people every day. It certainly doesn't hurt that, at least after the first few lean years of starting my own firm, I haven't had to worry about replacing the water heater when it breaks down. But what I love the most about being an insurance claims attorney is advocating for other people. Whether the people are consumers, hardworking business owners, representatives of an association, larger corporations, or a government entity, these "people" feel cheated and wronged by insurance companies exploiting the small print in policies in order to take advantage of policyholders. Now that my law practice has grown to have numerous offices in many states from coast to coast, we get to advocate for a whole lot of policyholders with all kinds of insurance problems.

As my stature in the law community has grown, calls come in every day from people across the country wanting advice. Sometimes these calls are from policyholders who have survived terrible tragedies and can't get their due from the insurance company. Others are from businesses needing advice on getting the right insurance products and hiring the right insurance agent. Some calls are from public adjusters and other consumer advocates asking for advice on advocacy issues. I sometimes talk with insurance commissioners and people in various departments of insurance, as well as lawmakers, lobbyists, and policymakers, all of them wanting insight or advice on insurance claims practices and how to make insurance work when a claim is made.

My impetus for writing this book, as well as my blog, is to share some of my knowledge about insurance practices, especially insurance company practices that harm policyholders. Most people simply don't know much about insurance products, which are one of the most important classes of products all of us purchase. They certainly don't know, yet fear, what the insurance companies may do when a loss happens and a claim is made. Most people don't know about how the insurance industry has changed, often for the worse, over the last few decades. They also don't know about policyholder advocates like me offering resources and recourse for them.

In the following pages, you will learn about the hidden ways that insurance companies sometimes take advantage of their own customers. You'll learn about the toxic bad faith culture some insurance claims departments engage in as a matter of claims philosophy. Most importantly, you'll learn what to watch out for and how to protect and advocate for yourself.

My hope is that this book will help you understand where you stand, how to proceed in the claims process, and, most importantly, when to seek help with any insurance problems you face, whether on your own or with the businesses you work for.

CHAPTER 1

WHEN A COMPUTER DECIDES WHETHER YOU LIVE OR DIE

IN THE 1990s a young woman purchased a health insurance policy she saw advertised in the newspaper, which was a common way for people without employer-sponsored health insurance to find policies at the time. She was approved for coverage, and she sent in her first payment.

Everything seemed good until a few months later when her doctors billed the first major claim against the policy. She went to her gynecologist complaining about unusual menstrual pain and bleeding. She had experienced similar symptoms about nine months before. The last time, the doctor ran some tests to make sure there were no major issues and then treated her for cramps. This time was different. This time the lab work came back showing an elevated white blood cell count. They ordered more testing and ultimately diagnosed her with an aggressive form of ovarian cancer. She needed surgery *immediately* to have the tumor removed—there was no time to wait. The cancer could metastasize at any moment, if it hadn't already, and at that point there might be no saving her.

Her doctors arranged the surgery and sought preapproval from the insurance company. To her horror, the claim was denied. The insurance company labeled the cancer a preexisting condition because she had experienced similar symptoms many months before buying the policy. Her health insurance excluded coverage for preexisting conditions, which was common before the Affordable Care Act mandated most standard health insurance plans cover preexisting conditions.

Without getting political about health care, the insurance company had this policy excluding preexisting conditions for a reason. They didn't want people to wait to get sick before signing up for health insurance. For the same reason you can't buy a fire insurance policy while your house is burning down or a flood insurance policy while the water is rising and about to start seeping in under the doorways, health insurance companies don't want to sell a policy that covers conditions you already have.

Preexisting condition clauses force people to stay insured. If pre-existing conditions are covered and people are free to buy policies whenever they want, people will just wait until they get sick to buy health insurance and cancel the policy after receiving treatment. The only people with insurance will be those sick people trying to get treatment. Under this scenario the price of health insurance would skyrocket. The Affordable Care Act gets around this problem by mandating that everyone carry insurance (or suffer a penalty) and restricting access to an enrollment period or qualifying event, such as when changing a job and losing employer-sponsored health insurance. Otherwise clauses excluding preexisting conditions would be necessary to keep the health insurance market from entering a death spiral.

In the young woman's case, the problem wasn't that her policy excluded preexisting conditions—the problem was that the cancer was *not* a preexisting condition! The symptoms she'd experienced before the policy was issued, while similar to the symptoms she was now experiencing, were not caused by the cancer. She'd had the same lab work done both times, and it only came back with positive indicators of ovarian cancer the second time. Her previous symptoms were from a hormonal imbalance. The cancer was new.

Her surgeon and gynecologist both wrote letters to the insurance company to explain that the two conditions, though presenting similarly, could not have been related. But the insurance company wouldn't budge. The system had made a determination that it was a preexisting condition. The insurance company refused to pay for the surgery.

This is when I learned about her case. Her lawyer reached out to me because he wanted his client to work with someone specializing in this type of law. I limit my practice to insurance claim disputes and do not do personal injury or any other type of law. I agreed to take on her case, but legal battles take time—time she did not have. She needed the surgery immediately. Thankfully her surgeon and the hospital were sympathetic. They agreed to perform the surgery and provide the operating room without charging her first.

She had the lifesaving surgery and was put on chemotherapy and radiation therapy. While her health was beginning to recover, her financial troubles were just beginning. She had to pay for the chemo and radiation treatments out of pocket. Her doctors again contacted the insurance company to explain that the biopsy from the surgery definitively proved that the cancer was new and not a preexisting condition. The insurance company still refused to pay.

At this point I felt that enough was enough, and we filed a lawsuit. As part of the discovery process, we requested her files from the insurance company. I will never forget what I saw scrawled into the margins of her insurance papers. Someone had written: "Help, help, help! It's obvious this was not a preexisting condition, but I can't get the computer to change its mind."

We later discovered that this was written by someone only after the lawsuit was filed. This was the first set of human eyes laid upon the insurance claim files. The person quickly realized the error but still couldn't get the software to correct the mistake!

I can't get the computer to change its mind.

I was immediately reminded of going to see Stanley Kubrick's film *2001: A Space Odyssey* as a child. In the movie a small crew conducts a space expedition to Jupiter in a spaceship with an advanced software system referred to as "HAL." The computer refers to itself as "foolproof and incapable of error," which echoes how insurance companies now talk about their automated systems. In the film, as with the insurance companies, this turns out to be untrue. HAL mistakenly decides that a mission-critical piece of equipment is malfunctioning due to human error. The crew knows that HAL is mistaken and that the equipment itself is actually malfunctioning on its own. Ultimately the astronauts decide to shut HAL down, but the computer discovers their plans and suffocates all the crew but one remaining person, Dave, who is outside of the ship at the time.

When Dave commands HAL to open the bay doors so that he can access the ship, HAL delivers the film's most famous line: "I'm sorry, Dave. I'm afraid I can't do that."

HAL had learned of the crew's plan to shut down the software and, thinking that it knows better, refuses to allow Dave to jeopardize the mission. This advanced software, now known as artificial intelligence or AI, is not being malevolent—to the contrary, it is trying to faithfully carry out the mission as it was programmed. But an error in that programming is now sabotaging the mission, and the crew has no way to fix the problem. The system has taken over.

This is conceptually similar to what happened to my client. The insurance company didn't have the right safeguards in place to make sure that the system was operating correctly. When it was finally brought to the claims department's attention, they *still* couldn't override the algorithm! Whoever had written that note in the margin of the report was powerless against the computer system and was begging a supervisor to help fix the problem. It didn't happen in time—and once the lawsuit was filed, they didn't want to own up to their mistake.

We eventually settled the case confidentially. The company paid for the surgery and issued a reimbursement for my client's chemo and radiation therapy. But the whole process put her through undue stress in a very trying time for no good reason. The entire problem could have been avoided if a real live human had taken the time to review the claim after a challenge was first issued. There was no reason for it to have to come to a lawsuit. The computer system was clearly at fault—it, like HAL, just couldn't see that fact.

These algorithms are now entrenched in the insurance and healthcare industries. They are used for *everything*. The human face of health care is a thin veneer. Everything you tell your doctor goes into the database. Every finding, every chart, every diagnosis, every prescription, every data point about your health—all of it gets coded and fed into the system. At that point, you become numbers that get plugged into a formula every time a decision about your health or

You may have the kindest, most attentive doctors in the world, but the insurance company claims system will still treat you like a set of codes.

coverage is made. You may have the kindest, most attentive doctors in the world, but the insurance company claims system will still treat you like a set of codes—because to the algorithms that make these critical decisions, that is exactly what you are.

The insurance company has a legal obligation to fully and clearly investigate every claim. But these "investigations," if you can call them that, are now being carried out by computers that cannot think for themselves. They are fed data from medical coders who often don't even read an entire document—they are trained to scan for keywords to punch into the system. Sometimes important contextual information gets dropped when diagnoses and modalities are reduced to codes. Sometimes, because the system is algorithmic and inflexible, the medical coders are forced to "fit a square peg into a round hole," and they leave out important information that the codes can't capture accurately.

I am not saying that the insurance industry should do away with data analytics and automated software. But we have removed the human element from critical decision-making, and that's a problem. Policyholders and patients need to understand how these decisions are made and be ready to question a claim that gets denied if the denial doesn't sound right, especially if that claim is for a "lifesaving procedure" or even just a life-changing amount of money. There's nothing worse than losing your life or health, but taking on the undue burden of ruinous medical debt has major negative impacts as well. Many studies show that medical expenses are one of the primary causes of bankruptcy in the United States, even among those who have health insurance.

WHAT WE NEED TO REALIZE ABOUT MODERN HEALTH INSURANCE

While close to 90 percent of US adults now have health insurance, few of them really understand the finer details of their policies. The majority of people don't have many options. Most working people obtain health insurance through their employer, who often offers only a few group options, if any options at all, from the same insurance company. People over sixty-five get Medicare, and those with limited incomes may get Medicaid, again with few options. College students obtain group policies through school. Only about 16 percent of the US population now purchases individual plans, which include plans bought on government-run exchanges, and even here most areas have few meaningful options.

Most people therefore choose a plan from limited options based on price, the deductible, co-pays, prescription coverage, and the provider network. For most people, that's all they really know about their plan. The fine print never gets read. Policyholders don't know how their policies actually work, and without meaningful options there is no apparent reason to learn before buying.

Policyholders are even more in the dark about how the insurance industry works behind the scenes. They don't know how prices get set, how people are lumped into coverage groups, and how claims get processed. No one considers claims processing until they have an important claim denied. We buy health insurance with the hope that we won't actually need it, at least not for catastrophic events. It is only after a catastrophic and expensive injury or illness, such as an accident or a cancer diagnosis, and a claim is denied that these finer details take a front-and-center presence in our lives.

Most people would be *very* surprised if they knew how their claims were processed. Technology has revolutionized how claims are processed—and not always for the better. Insurance companies have streamlined claims processing in order to slash costs as the industry has grown larger and larger. Health insurance is now so ubiquitous that you may assume it has always been this way—it has not. While accident and disability insurance has been around for over a century, the modern health insurance market only took off in the mid-twentieth century. Coverage of routine medical expenses is even more recent. People used to pay cash for prescriptions and doctors' visits. Insurance was primarily for catastrophic health problems. But as health insurance was marketed more aggressively, the industry grew into the mammoth system we have today.

This growth in coverage, both in terms of people and services covered, has caused costs to balloon. Insurance now covers doctors, specialists, prescriptions, labor and delivery, preventive care, and everything else *in addition* to emergencies, surgeries, and other catastrophic events. Add to that expensive cutting-edge medical technology and the fact that people are living longer, and costs have gone through the roof. Multiply those costs by the three hundred million Americans with health insurance and factor in the overhead costs of administration and infrastructure, and it is easy to see why health-care spending in the United States is now almost 20 percent of our gross domestic product.

By the 1990s the health-care industry *had* to start reducing costs. In a competitive market, the easiest thing to cut was administration costs, which had expanded dramatically with the increase in coverage. Historically, whenever a doctor, hospital, or pharmacy billed insurance for a procedure, someone at the insurance company would process the claim and ensure that it was covered by the policy. As part of claims processing, insurance companies must determine what treatments and modalities, which is health-care jargon for methods of diagnosis (e.g., exams, imaging, and lab work), are covered under a plan. With the rise in coverage, paying people to process all these claims was becoming not just expensive but actually infeasible. Billions of claims must be processed each year, totaling trillions of dollars, and while over 90 percent of these claims are eventually approved, each one has to be considered—or at least that's how it used to work once upon a time.

Increasingly, the insurance industry has turned toward automation to process claims more quickly, efficiently, and *affordably*. The shift from people processing claims to software started in the 1960s and 1970s as business computers became more common in the workplace and really accelerated throughout the 1980s and 1990s as cheap personal computers became prevalent. Today health insurance claims processing is almost completely automated and performed by a computer algorithm programmed to do the job that used to be done by real live human beings. Health providers and insurance providers employ medical "coders" to translate diagnoses and treatments into standardized codes that can be fed into the insurance company's payment system. The coders go over the doctor's charts, notes, and forms and translate them into medical jargon. This code is then automatically transferred onto bills and sent to the insurer claims department, where software will verify that the codes correspond to covered care under the policyholder's plan. If the code is valid, the software pays the bill—if not, the claim is rejected.

> Today health insurance claims processing is almost completely automated and performed by a computer algorithm programmed to do the job that used to be done by real live human beings.

Now, I am not against automation. Automated systems have advantages. There are trillions of processes that must be approved, monitored, and tracked across the health-care industry every day. Humans aren't capable of managing such a large, complex system without computer assistance. Software allows claims to be processed faster, which means bills are paid more quickly. Automation also creates organized and clean data that can be used for analytics to improve service and inform business processes. And automation really does cut costs. Insurance companies no longer have to employ an army of claims processors. They only have to pay for the software and a much smaller group of medical coders. Software doesn't take a salary, call in sick, request vacations, or require training. This cuts costs, and, in a competitive health-care market, much of the savings gets passed on to the consumer.

But problems arise when automated cost-cutting measures don't include proper quality control performed by actual humans. Automated systems are often touted as being unsusceptible to human error. This is only true once the codes have been fed into the system, as medical coders can still make human errors. Even more problematic, though, are errors with the algorithms themselves. Humans can *think*. Despite recent advances in AI, computers don't really think—they only run algorithms as told. Algorithms are good at accurately executing functions and analyzing large data sets, but they are not able to evaluate context and conditions that the algorithm doesn't account for. And if the software doesn't have the proper human oversight, errors entered into or introduced by the algorithm will propagate through the system. As they say in Silicon Valley: garbage in, garbage out. Computers lack the critical judgment and nuanced reasoning necessary to detect special cases and even obvious inconsistencies. Computers can't make nuanced decisions about the intent of the providers or medical coders—only humans can do that.

Most policyholders don't realize that once the medical coders input the claim into the system, it is rare for an actual set of human eyes to ever gaze upon their files again. This is a real problem when you have computer algorithms making "life or death" decisions about people's health. Without human oversight and the ability for real humans to easily correct mistakes and errors in processing, claims can and do get rejected when they should not.

HOW TO PROTECT YOURSELF

We are all mortal. We all get old. Every last one of us will get sick someday. That is why everyone should carry health insurance. But as we have seen, just getting coverage doesn't mean that your treatments will be covered. Not all valid claims are accepted. Insurance companies have obli-

> **Many claim denials are made in error, and the insurance company has no incentive to advocate for your case unless you do.**

gations to their policyholders, but sometimes you have to fight to make sure those obligations are kept.

Here is how you can advocate for yourself:

First, don't just accept what the insurance company tells you. If something seems wrong, it probably is. Many claim denials are made in error, and the insurance company has no incentive to advocate for your case unless you do. The insurance company isn't necessarily acting in bad faith. In the case of health insurance, an actual person may not have evaluated the claim.

Second, understand that virtually all business processes and decisions are influenced by automated systems. You have to go *above* the system to get your case fully investigated by a person with authority to correct the problem. The people who answer phones are real people, but they are not decision makers—they generally just use the system. When you call about your claim, they will simply look you up in the system and tell you what you already know—that the system denied your claim. They usually don't even have the authority to question the system. You want to speak to people who can make actual decisions and override the software.

In other words, HAL won't fix the problem for you. HAL is the problem. You need to talk to Dave.

Ask to speak to a manager—then ask to speak to the manager's supervisor. Work your way up the ladder until you get an actual decision maker on the phone. With persistence, you can often find an officer or director on the phone. This person can help you. John Doe or Susie Q answering phones most likely cannot.

Third, don't be afraid to get help navigating the system. Contrary to common advice, you are not always your best advocate. Lawyers are keen on reminding people that they have a fool for a client when they represent themselves. This applies to insurance disputes as well. The average policyholder does not know insurance laws and regulations or how the insurance claims system works. When dealing with matters of "life or death" or situations involving substantial amounts of money, you probably want to get a specialist involved who understands the system.

Even experts can struggle to get an insurance company to change its position quickly. One of the attorneys in my law firm, Rene Sigman, found this out the hard way when her young son, Blake, was diagnosed with anaplastic large-cell lymphoma, or ALCL, a rare, aggressive cancer, in October 2015. Rene specializes in insurance law. Day in and day out, she advocates for policyholders and those fighting to get lifesaving treatments covered. Now, she was that policyholder. She was advocating for her own family.

Blake was very sick. He spent months in the hospital after his diagnosis. The cancer compromised his immune system, causing a lung infection that threatened his breathing. He slipped into a ten-day coma. His family wasn't sure that he would make it. Fortunately the chemotherapy eventually worked, and Blake came out of his coma. But the treatment caused its own nasty side effects, including a pulmonary embolism and a collapsed lung. He still couldn't go home. They spent the holidays at the hospital.

Things didn't start to turn around until after the New Year. Blake underwent six rounds of chemotherapy before he was finally declared cancer-free. Tragically, his remission didn't last long. A few months later, while Blake was back at the hospital, he discovered a lump on his neck. When he showed the lump to Rene, her heart sank. Their worst fears were soon confirmed. The cancer had returned, quickly and aggressively, and by Easter, Blake was back in the hospital full time again.

Blake desperately needed a bone marrow transplant, but the procedure couldn't be performed until his cancer was back in remission. His other treatments weren't working. His best bet, according to their doctors, was a new experimental drug developed specifically for his rare cancer. The treatment worked rapidly in clinical trials and was shown to have an 85 percent success rate. Unfortunately the clinical trials were already closed, and the drug was not yet FDA approved and widely available.

Rene and her team jumped into action. The drug was new and expensive, and because it was for a rare disease, the only pharmacy that kept it in stock was in Indiana. Rene and Blake lived in Houston. Rene called Pfizer, the manufacturer, to request the drug directly, but they wouldn't release it to Texas Children's Hospital in Houston because the hospital didn't have the necessary license for the experimental treatment. Their only hope was to get the drug from the pharmacy in Southern Indiana.

Rene got on the phone with both the pharmacy and her insurance company. Even though she had Blake covered under a premier "Cadillac" health plan, the insurance company refused to pay for the drug because the only pharmacy that had it available wasn't an approved pharmacy. She was supposed to buy it from a specialty pharmacy, but they didn't even have the drug on hand, and there was no time to waste. Rene would have to pay for the prescription out of pocket for now, which would cost $27,000, if she could even get the pharmacy to authorize it. This was no easy task. The pharmacy was not a retail pharmacy and generally didn't do private sales. They mostly supplied hospitals. Rene spent hours on the phone with different people from the pharmacy, pleading with them to dispense the drug, until she got an angel of a woman on the other end of the line who promised to help. She was a mother, too, and said that she couldn't sleep at night knowing Blake's story. She came through the next day with the authorization for a direct private sale of the experimental drug.

The pharmacy promised to ship the drugs overnight to Houston, but this wasn't fast enough. Time was of the essence. Blake was very ill, and his condition was deteriorating. By pure serendipity, Rene had family in Southern Indiana who could pick up the drugs before the pharmacy closed. Even more fortunately, Rene's former employer agreed to fly another family member out to Indiana to pick up the drugs. That evening, Rene had the pills in hand, and Blake took his first dose late that night. They proved to be literal miracle drugs. Blake had been teetering on the edge of death when he swallowed the first pills. Within two days, he was well enough to be discharged from the hospital.

As a mother, Rene was thankful that her son was able to access the lifesaving drugs that he so direly needed; however, professionally, as an advocate for others, she felt outraged by the whole ordeal. There were miracle drugs that could save a child's life, and she had had to fight a system that largely didn't care. Rene was well aware of her own personal privilege that had made getting the drug possible. She was able to take time off work to be with Blake and stay on the phone with the pharmacy and manufacturer for days. She was able to pay $27,000 out of pocket for a handful of pills and wait to fight the insurance company for a reimbursement later, when she wasn't also fighting for her son's life. She was able to speak English, but many of the other parents in the cancer wing of the children's hospital could not, nor do many of her clients, and doing so is necessary to be able to communicate with the right people.

Above all Rene is a brilliant attorney who works in insurance law. She knew the system and how to navigate it. She knew whom to call and what to say. She knew not to take no for an answer and how to eventually finagle a yes from the right person. She had the skills and the know-how to advocate for her son in a way that the vast majority of parents unskilled in insurance law cannot.

Few of our clients, faced with the same situation as Rene, would stand a chance on their own. Most people don't have the skill set, insider knowledge, education, and experience to navigate the insurance claims system the way she did. Most other parents in her situation would have had to watch their child die, knowing full well that there were lifesaving drugs locked away in a pharmacy somewhere. She shudders to think about it.

I tell Rene's story here since, even with all her privileges and luck, she succeeded because she did three things right. One, she didn't take no for an answer and instead advocated for herself. Two, she went up and over the system repeatedly to make the impossible possible. Three, she got an expert involved—*herself*.

If you find yourself in similar straits, don't be afraid to reach out to consumer advocates and attorneys. There are lawyers who focus only on helping policyholders with insurance disputes. There are even lawyers who specialize only in *health* insurance. You don't always need the cash to pay them up front. Depending on the nature of your claim, many policyholder attorneys will work on a contingency fee basis so that you do not have to pay out of pocket unless they win.

CHAPTER 2

ROCK YOU LIKE A HURRICANE—AND THEN BLOCK YOU

THE INSURANCE POLICY SMALL PRINT

RAY AND ANN STIEFFEL are a "salt of the earth" couple from Bay St. Louis, Mississippi. I first met them and their twelve children in 1970, after my father was transferred to work on monster-size sea buoys to help predict weather and aid in sea navigation.

The year before, Category 5 hurricane Camille ravaged Bay St. Louis and neighboring towns on the Mississippi Gulf Coast. To this day, I can recall the water lines from Camille's storm surge on our rented home in Waveland, Mississippi, and other instances on unrepaired structures. The Stieffels are our Mississippi friends who recite countless stories about surviving Hurricane Camille, which was considered the worst modern era hurricane until 2005, when Hurricane Katrina stunned the Mississippi coast.

After Hurricane Katrina, we represented a number of car dealerships along the Mississippi coast and were retained to provide advice to these insurance claimants. As we flew over the devastated areas, I said, "It looks like God blew in and washed away everything close to the coastline."

Ray and Ann Stieffel decided to ride out that storm. They, and many of their neighbors, remembered when the storm surge waters stopped during Hurricane Camille. The Stieffels judged their safety based upon what they thought was the ultimate hurricane. These memories proved deadly for many others, and the Stieffels were lucky to escape.

Hurricanes are getting stronger and more common. Global warming, whether or not the result of human activity, is heating up the oceans. Warmer oceans make for stronger storms and longer hurricane seasons. Add to that the fact that more people are living and working on the coasts than ever means that these storms are only going to get deadlier, more destructive, and *costlier* going forward.

Hurricane Katrina brought unprecedented levels of destruction that few anticipated. Even knowing that Katrina was a Category 5 during its approach, people living a few miles inland underestimated the storm. Though graded by wind speed, hurricanes often cause the most damage through flooding. The older folks in these inland communities who remembered Hurricane Camille in 1969 could point to where the waterline had stopped rising in their town. Camille's storm surge peaked at twenty-four feet, the highest on record until Katrina, and residents such as the Stieffels, whose homes were above the 1969 waterline, believed they were safe. They found out differently. As Katrina came ashore, communities like Pass Christian, Mississippi, saw storm surges as high as twenty-eight feet, a good four feet over what Camille had brought.

During our initial visit, the highways were lined with cars on the shoulders of the roads and down in the ditches. At first I thought these were volunteers who had come to help. They were not. We quickly realized that some people who waited too long to evacuate got caught in floodwaters and had their cars washed off the road. Having previously lived in the area, I was heartbroken to see familiar communities all but washed off the map. Many people who stayed lost their lives. There is still no exact count of casualties.

At the Stieffel home, the water kept rising and entering the house. Ray and Ann moved up into the attic. When water started filling the attic, they were trapped. With nowhere to go, they busted through the attic vent and clawed their way out of the house. The water was up to the roof. They held on to tree branches to keep from being washed away, bobbing up and down in the floodwaters until the storm surge receded. By the time they could stand without being swept away, the water had washed the clothes off their backs and their house had been washed away. They had to go into their neighbors' homes to scavenge for clothes. They were lucky to be alive, but their lives were the only thing that had been spared. Everything they owned was gone.

Coming back from this type of loss is not easy. Ann and Ray, though past retirement age, were still working. Losing your home and everything else always takes a heavy toll. A home is your castle, and at that age starting from scratch can be daunting, if not impossible.

In the days after the storm, Ray often visited the place where their house had stood. There was nothing left behind but a concrete slab marking the spot like a tombstone. At their age, for most people, this kind of loss is life altering without adequate insurance coverage. The emotional toll of such an ordeal cannot be overstated.

Unfortunately Ray and Ann did not have much flood insurance, only about $25,000 of coverage. Like many unsuspecting policyholders, they believed "flood coverage" was for people living in floodplains. They never considered flooding from a storm surge during a hurricane.

Most people think of that as a hurricane event, not a flooding event.

Few private insurance carriers cover flooding, and it is almost never included in basic homeowners policies. Most people get flood insurance through the National Flood Insurance Program, a government program that covers houses in flood-prone areas that private insurers won't cover on their own. Unfortunately many people think that their homeowners insurance policy speaks for all hurricane damage. This is often not the case.

> Unfortunately many people think that their homeowners insurance policy speaks for all hurricane damage. This is often not the case.

While Ray and Ann did not have much flood insurance, they did have plenty of homeowners coverage. Since their house was severely damaged by *both* wind and water, one would assume that they would still get significant money for the wind damage, especially because Hurricane Katrina produced sustained winds of 125 miles per hour. However, the insurance company refused to pay for either, citing, within the small print, what is known as an anti-concurrent causation (ACC) clause.

ACC CLAUSES AND SLAB CASES

Though few policyholders are aware of them, the ACC clause became standard language in most "all-risk" homeowner insurance policies starting in the early 1990s. Calling these policies "all-risk" is something of a misnomer, as they typically include exclusions, such as for flooding. When a structure suffers both covered losses (e.g., from wind) and from excluded causes (e.g., flooding) concurrently, the insurance company must decide how much damage is attributable to each source. This creates a conflict that encourages insurance carriers to attribute more damage to excluded causes while understating covered claims, a practice that has resulted in substantial litigation. To sidestep the issue entirely, many insurance carriers adopted ACC provisions that exclude covered losses when they occur concurrently with excluded causes. In plain terms, this means that a policy covering wind will not pay claims for wind damage if there is concurrent flood damage that is excluded. The result is devastating for many hurricane victims. Wind damage only? You get paid. Wind damage plus water damage? You get nothing.

Hurricanes can often create storm surges that wash away whole structures. We call these "slab cases," so named for the concrete foundation left behind. Slab cases leave no evidence behind to determine how much was damaged by wind or how much was damaged by floodwater.

In the Stieffels' case, there was almost nothing left of their home to prove the amount of wind damage, just the concrete slab. The wind *had* damaged their home, but the water destroyed all the evidence. So while they had been paying for years on a policy that provided "hurricane coverage," the insurance company refused to pay for any wind damage due to the storm surge flooding.

Their case is not unique. Thousands of their neighbors were given the same reason for denial. While a few states have declared ACC provisions unenforceable, many states, including Mississippi, had not ruled on the issue prior to Hurricane Katrina. Eventually the Mississippi Supreme Court ruled, in another slab case known as the *Corban* case, that ACC clauses do not apply to most claims dealing with hurricanes. The ruling now requires insurance companies to prove how much damage was caused solely by flooding.

While this is a simplification of the ruling, it captures its spirit.

Every case is unique, and each state has its own laws, regulations, and judicial precedents. But the *Corban* case shows that policyholders can fight back against unfair denials and win. Over time, insurance claims attorneys, including me, have found ways to help "slabbed" victims obtain full recovery. When the law isn't written to favor the insurance company, the policyholder can win. After all, the insurance company is faced with the same lack of evidence. Most states, with the exception of Texas, now require insurance companies to prove how much damage is excluded under typical homeowners policies.

THE OTHER FINE PRINT

ACC clauses aren't the only fine print policyholders may run afoul of, nor does your house have to be "slabbed" for the insurance company to find reasons not to pay your claim. Insurance companies have denied claims for all kinds of bizarre and nonsensical reasons. Damage that should be covered can get misreported, undervalued, or excluded in many ways.

A couple in Puerto Rico whom we represented had their claim denied on a bizarre technicality that didn't even apply to them. They were retired. He worked as an electrical engineer. She was a homemaker. They built their dream home on the side of a mountain in Ponce, on the southern side of the island. They raised chickens and gardened out back. When I visited to assess the damage and get to know them personally, as I like to do with clients, she brewed fresh coffee from beans that neighbors had grown.

They recounted the story of the devastating storm, Hurricane Maria, that wrecked their home. The building had started shaking in the wind. Terrified that the house would blow over, they locked themselves in the bathroom and prayed. While the structure withstood the storm, the wind blew out the skylight, and rainwater came into the house. They had six inches of water damage on all the walls, and the floors were ruined. The frame was good, but they had to gut much of the interior.

This damage should have been covered. Their policy excluded damage from water that seeped in around natural openings, as sometimes happens due to the massive pressure a hurricane produces, but that wasn't what happened. The wind breached the structure by blowing out the skylight. Water damage that resulted from wind damage *was* covered by their policy. But the insurance company treated the water damage the same way they would have if debris clogged the gutters and backed water onto the roof, where it could seep into vents and around cracks. Their claim should have been paid immediately. Instead they were given an obscure and nonsensical reason why the claim was denied on a technicality that didn't even apply to their situation.

Making sense of the sometimes bizarre methodology that insurance companies use to assess claims will make your head spin.

Making sense of the sometimes bizarre methodology that insurance companies use to assess claims will make your head spin. Their logic often defies common sense. For example, we represented hundreds of people on the Bolivar Peninsula in Texas after Hurricane Ike blew through in 2008. Many people had their wind claims systematically underpaid. The Texas Windstorm Insurance Association (TWIA), which insured the vast majority of houses on the peninsula, determined that the wind had only caused 11 percent of the damage *for everyone*, as if all cases were the same, all buildings the same, all damage the same. This was not the case. There was no scientific or logical reason to expect that it would be.

My friend Tom Grail came up with the parable of Hurricane Ike insurance claims to capture the absurdity of the situation. It goes like this: Larry and Moe were both on the Bolivar Peninsula when Hurricane Ike hit. Larry was struck in the head by airborne debris and then swept away by the storm surge but survived by clinging to floating timber. The doctors who treated his injuries attributed 11 percent of them to the airborne debris. Moe, not so lucky, was killed instantly by a flying TV set and swept away in the storm surge. When his body was recovered, the medical examiners determined that the wind was only 11 percent responsible for his injuries because that was what happened to Larry. If this sounds absurd, then you can see how TWIA's methodology for assessing claims had no basis in science or reality.

Cases such as this are sometimes the result of a legitimate misunderstanding or systemic error. However, they can be the result of bad faith on the part of insurance companies trying to minimize payouts by denying legitimate claims.

AND THEN THERE IS FRAUD ...

Insurance companies have been caught fabricating evidence and altering reports to lower what they pay in claims. When a claim is made against a property insurance policy, the insurance company sends out engineers to conduct a survey. Engineering reports are then used to assess damage and determine whether losses are covered or excluded by the policy. While most people are honest, insurance companies have an incentive to pressure engineers to minimize the amount of covered damage they include in reports. They also have an incentive to pressure claims adjusters to revise reports down even further.

We once represented a woman, married to a doctor, who was present when the engineer surveyed her home after Hurricane Katrina. Although the engineer told her he saw significant wind damage, the final report that came back from the insurance company cited almost no wind damage. She called the engineer at his home and read him the report. He was shocked. Someone had altered his report.

We obtained his copy of the original report as well as dozens of other reports he had written for the same company. Many of these cases turned into lawsuits, and the whole thing became a big scandal. The insurance company had been systematically falsifying engineering reports. They were minimizing wind damage and overstating flood damage, effectively passing the buck to the National Flood Insurance Program. Policyholders, unlikely to scrutinize reports as long as losses were somehow covered, were mostly none the wiser. The ultimate victim, in most cases, was not the policyholder but the taxpayer. National Flood Insurance is a public program, and it was being duped into overpaying for flooding.

This was not an isolated case. Other insurers did the very same thing. After Hurricane Katrina, State Farm systematically pressured engineers to overstate flood damage and ignore or minimize wind damage. Two claims adjusters, the Rigsby sisters, famously blew the whistle and brought a qui tam lawsuit (i.e., a suit in which they could receive a portion of the penalties levied against the defendant in exchange for their cooperation). The case made its way to the US Supreme Court, where a ruling against the insurance company was upheld, but legal proceedings continue to this day.

Court rulings such as this were a win for policyholders, but they resulted in an overcorrection. Following the 2005 Hurricane Katrina scandal, the National Flood Insurance Program began scrutinizing claims more carefully. Engineers and estimators who had been previously pressured to overstate water damage were now being overly conservative in their assessments. Once their reports or estimates were sent to the insurance company, they were often changed or reduced by other claims adjusters, resulting in denials or reductions in how much would be paid—often by as much as 30 percent. Not wanting to get hit with an audit and assessed penalties, they were being cautious and sometimes fraudulent.

This resulted in thousands of lawsuits and yet another scandal following Hurricane Sandy in 2012. This time the National Flood Insurance Program and its contracted insurers systematically *underpaid* water damage. In these cases, policyholders were more likely to notice because they did not receive payment in full for their losses. My firm represented at least eight hundred such cases after Hurricane Sandy. This was a big change. After Hurricane Ike, only four years before, we could count the number of our cases in which flood damage was underpaid by National Flood Insurance Program adjusters on one hand.

In the most egregious cases after Hurricane Sandy, the National Flood Insurance Program underestimated water damage while private insurers underpaid for wind damage. Such problems are, again, mostly the result of the incentive created by having multiple insurers offering coverage for separate damages that often occur concurrently. A better solution would be to have more hurricane policies that cover both flooding and wind damage. With only one insurer involved, there is no incentive to play games over what caused the damage because the same carrier pays for both perils.

Unfortunately such policies are almost never available. Very few private insurance companies offer flood insurance on the open market, which is why Congress established the National Flood Insurance Program in 1968. Flooding is a peril closely associated with large geographic areas. The homeowners most likely to buy flood insurance are those who are most likely to experience flooding. Yet people forgo flood insurance entirely. Large catastrophic damages over a large geographic area make it difficult for private insurance companies to offer flood insurance at affordable prices. As a result, the federal government had to step in and do the job while leaving wind damage to be covered entirely by private insurers.

HOW TO PROTECT YOURSELF

Until comprehensive policies that cover both wind and water become the norm, homeowners and business owners must protect themselves with the tools currently at their disposal. There *are* measures you can take to protect yourself now.

First, do not assume you are safe from flooding. Global warming is creating stronger and more frequent hurricanes, and storm surges are coming farther inland. Strong hurricanes can also dump massive amounts of rain over large areas when they hover in one place, as was recently the case with Hurricane Harvey in Texas, where a state of emergency was declared over thirty counties. Those who do not live in flood-prone areas should still consider buying flood insurance, which is much cheaper in areas that are not prone to flooding.

Second, do not assume flood damage is covered under your standard homeowners or business owners policy—it rarely is. Many people believe that windstorm coverage, which some insurance agents might refer to as "hurricane insurance," covers losses not caused by the storm surge. Again, this is rarely the case. Policyholders must typically buy a separate policy specifically for flood coverage in order to have the insurance company pay for flooding damage from a hurricane and its storm surge.

Third, invest in as much flood insurance as possible to cover your entire exposure. The National Flood Insurance Program only covers a maximum $250,000 in losses for residential structures and $500,000 for commercial buildings. Home and business values often exceed these figures. Some insurance companies offer what is known as "excess flood insurance" that will cover losses over and above your National Flood Insurance coverage. Businesses can also buy "difference in conditions" policies, which are often more inclusive of perils and tend to offer higher limits. While flood insurance isn't standard in most policies, you can often find the coverage that you need through knowledgeable insurance agents.

Never accept "no coverage" for an answer without getting a second opinion.

Fourth, understand the ins and outs of your policies. Be an informed consumer. Know what you are entitled to under your policy. In most states there are limitations on how the insurance company can apply exclusions to coverage—but you may need an attorney to argue your case. If your insurance claim is being denied on what seems like a technicality or unfair exclusion, it is possible that your insurer may be in the wrong. Never accept "no coverage" for an answer without getting a second opinion. A skilled insurance coverage attorney may be able to help you get unfairly denied claims paid.

CHAPTER 3

ZOMBIES, GHOSTS, AND EVERYONE ELSE

HOW PARANOIA OVER FRAUD ENSNARES HONEST POLICYHOLDERS

IN THE 1990s I started to get involved in life insurance cases due to the AIDS epidemic. Many gay men were purchasing life insurance for fear of contracting HIV. The insurance companies vetted these people closely before issuing policies to be sure they weren't already sick. These cases received so much scrutiny that beneficiaries often had their claims declared fraudulent on the grounds that the policyholder was already sick when purchasing the policy.

While there probably were some such cases, many gay men simply bought policies because they understood their future risk. There were few effective antiviral treatments at the time. Transmission was more common, and infection was more of a death sentence. The problem wasn't rampant fraud—the problem was an uncontrolled public health epidemic. Paranoia over fraud resulted in legitimate claims being scrutinized and denied.

Of course, legitimate fraud does happen, and we see it occasionally. My work with these life insurance cases resulted in a man being referred to me for help with a claim made against his deceased grandfather's life insurance policy. The prospective client was a Haitian man living in the Little Haiti neighborhood of Miami, home to many Caribbean immigrants. He was the beneficiary on his grandfather's policy, but the insurance company denied the claim because they wanted more proof that his grandfather had actually died.

I didn't understand. "Proof? Didn't he have a funeral?"

"Yes."

"Were people there? Didn't they see his body?"

"Yes."

"Is there a death certificate?"

"Yes."

His English was not good. He spoke in broken sentences. I suspected that the insurance company was trying to take advantage of a vulnerable person. After taking on his case, I followed up with the insurance company. They wouldn't budge. They insisted that there wasn't sufficient documentation of the death and wanted more proof before approving the claim.

The case was headed for a lawsuit. In preparation for court, I collected documentation of the death. We gathered the death certificate, photographs from the funeral, bills for the funeral services, names and contact information for people who had attended the service, and more. It looked like a simple open-and-shut case.

Around this time, I got a call from Diego Asencio, a lawyer in Palm Beach, Florida. He wanted me to join him as co-counsel on a bad faith case against State Farm. We started talking about some of the other cases we were working on, and he mentioned having problems with what was now this *third* life insurance case involving Haitians in

Miami. My heart jumped when he said this. Three cases? There were only a few thousand people in Little Haiti, and it seemed odd to have so many life insurance claims in such a small community. The LGBT community was larger and facing a deadly epidemic—why would so many Haitians in this one area of Miami be filing claims? My internal alarm was going off.

I pushed for details. Diego said that the insurance company wanted proof that the policyholder was actually deceased. They were so skeptical that they actually wanted to exhume the body! This seemed crazy to me, but he explained that there had been a spate of insurance fraud cases in Little Haiti involving faked deaths. Some of these scams were very elaborate. A little cottage industry had sprung up around them. There were people selling fake birth certificates and holding funerals for people who hadn't died and sometimes had never even existed.

My jaw kept dropping as he spoke. This sounded so much like my own case that I feared my client was also engaging in fraud. Too embarrassed to tell Diego, I said my goodbyes and immediately started digging into my case.

I try to maintain a healthy skepticism about every case when something doesn't add up, but the man had seemed so sincere and had so much evidence. But the case started to fall apart as we dug into it. The insurance company hadn't met with the policyholder before issuing the policy. The policy was for $50,000. For such a small policy, they didn't send someone out to evaluate the policyholder, give him an exam, and do lab work as they would for a larger policy. They just wrote him a policy and started collecting the premiums. When I looked for more information on the grandfather, nothing came up. There was the death certificate but no birth certificate. There were no other records of him at all. It was like he was a ghost.

I called Diego back later to follow up on his case. "Did they exhume the body?"

"Yeah, Chip," he said, laughing over the phone. "They dug up the grave. We have a zombie on our hands."

"What do you mean a zombie?"

"They dug up the grave. It was empty," he said. "He must have gotten up and walked out!"

We were both cracking up at this point. I fessed up about my own case finally and told him about my "ghost."

I dropped the case right away. As a civil attorney, I do not deal with any kind of fraud. We are an upstanding law firm with strong principles and a reputation to protect. We ethically had to drop the case.

A CULTURE OF PARANOIA

Cases of legitimate fraud such as this do happen, but they are relatively rare. Most claims are made by honest policyholders. But that is not the story you hear from insurance associations, which paint a picture of rampant fraud. The Insurance Information Institute claims that 10 percent of all property and casualty losses are the result of insurance fraud. Their website claims that this translated into an annual loss of $30 billion between 2013 and 2017, the same figure they have been quoting for years, for the insurance industry. Some insurance spokespersons have suggested that fraud costs the average American household $5,000 extra in premiums each year, a figure that seems suspect given that the average inflation-adjusted household income over the last few decades has ranged from about $50,000 to $60,000, depending on how you calculate it. The notion that insurance fraud costs Americans 10 percent of their pretax income seems dubious, to say the least.

The insurance industry has a vested interest in putting forth this story about rampant fraud. Whenever insurance fraud does occur, the insurance industry public relations departments do everything in their power to publicize it. This gives the impression that insurance fraud is more common than it actually is.

One way to interpret this behavior is as paranoia. The insurance industry has whipped itself into a frenzy to root out fraud. They are so fearful of getting ripped off that they see fraud everywhere, even where it is not, and publicizing cases of fraud provides a powerful deterrent. Publicizing arrests and lengthy criminal sentencing sends a message to would-be scammers to think twice before trying to commit insurance fraud.

A more cynical interpretation, though no less positive, is that the insurance industry is engaged in a conspiracy to cast doubt on its own customers. Overstating the prevalence of fraud allows the industry to lobby for policies that favor insurance carriers over the consumer. Scary statistics suggesting that 10 percent of claims are fraudulent give lobbyists and regulators a justification for trying to roll back consumer protections. The perception of rampant fraud helps sway regulators, politicians, and even the general public. It also gives claims adjusters more leeway to scrutinize each and every claim that comes in.

As the saying goes: to a hammer, everything looks like a nail. These SIUs often see fraud where there is none.

Which is exactly what is happening. Most insurance companies now have special investigative units (SIUs) staffed with claim adjusters specially trained to identify fraud. There's nothing inherently wrong with this, but these adjusters and investigators spend all their time looking for and thinking about fraud. As the saying goes: to a hammer, everything looks like a nail. These SIUs often see fraud where there is none. Throwing out a net wide enough to catch every case of fraud means that some honest policyholders get reeled in as collateral damage. Sometimes fraud is even used as an excuse to deny claims that are clearly legitimate.

We see honest policyholders running afoul of these anti-fraud policies more than we see actual fraud. An insurer was once convinced that one of my clients was trying to commit insurance fraud simply because she was eccentric and her story unusual. She was a middle-aged woman into New Age spirituality. She lived in Florida but took trips to North Carolina to collect gemstones in the mountains. While she was away on one of these trips, her apartment was broken into and various items were stolen, including many of her gemstones. She believed there was someone stalking her, a Peeping Tom whom she claimed to have seen using a pair of binoculars to watch her getting dressed through the window. The insurance company found this story suspicious, partly because there was no sign of forced entry but probably more because they found her kooky.

Her claim was denied due to "material misrepresentation" in the statements she made after the loss. She had been asked to report the value of her stolen belongings under oath, which is common practice when the insurance company suspects a claim might be fraudulent. They sent one of these SIU adjusters trained in fraud detection to administer an investigation and collect the statement. They took issue with the value she ascribed to some of her gemstones. Some were worth pennies or a few dollars, but others were, according to her, worth hundreds. They all looked more or less the same, but she claimed that some had magical powers, making them valuable.

Now, I was, of course, skeptical about these supposed magical powers. But when I met her in person, it was clear she honestly believed that the "magic" gemstones were special. She showed me some different gemstones and explained how some gave off auras. She was adamant in this claim, a true believer. She was no con artist. She just wanted the insurance company to pay what she believed the stones were worth. I didn't believe this kind of hocus-pocus, and neither did the insurance company, but *she* did, and that's what matters when determin-

The insurer doesn't have to accept your opinion, but as long as you don't intentionally misrepresent the value, you haven't committed fraud.

ing fraud. Fraud is a crime of intent. You are allowed to state your honest opinion about the value of your losses. The insurer doesn't have to accept your opinion, but as long as you don't intentionally misrepresent the value, you haven't committed fraud.

In her case, she had clearly explained why she believed the gemstones were valuable. The insurance company didn't like her reasons, but that doesn't make her statements fraudulent. Would I pay $500 for a gemstone? No. But I also wouldn't pay $100 to see a so-called psychic, and people do that every day, so her claims weren't out of line.

While she may have been a little delusional by many standards, she wasn't harming anybody, and she certainly wasn't trying to commit fraud. She was not trying to misrepresent the value of the stones. She had been meticulous in cataloging them and explaining their worth. Those are not the actions of a con artist. A simpler and better con would have been to claim lost electronics and jewelry without making up a convoluted story about a Peeping Tom and magic gemstones.

Being eccentric does not change the fact that she had been paying on her insurance policy for nine years. The insurance company just wanted to deny her claim outright by alleging fraud. That's not fair—and it's not good customer service. If she wasn't too kooky for them to collect her payments for all those years, then she shouldn't have been too kooky to be taken seriously after a claim was made. She was a loyal and honest customer, and there was no good defense for dragging her name through the mud. I see this all the time, often in less peculiar cases, where the insurance company is happy to collect premiums but then turns on its own customers as soon as a claim is made.

I took on her case. I was up front about not believing in her theory regarding the stalker and the magical gemstones, but that didn't mean I couldn't help. The insurance company was doing her wrong and making serious allegations against her without cause. While she didn't exactly like my honesty, she believed I could help. She liked that my surname is Merlin, the name of the famous wizard in the King Arthur tales, which she took as a sign of otherworldly intervention. (This is probably the only time I have been hired for my mystical associations.)

We first had to show that the apartment could have been broken into. The insurance company made a big deal about there being no pry marks on the door or doorframe to suggest forced entry. I hired a security professional to look at the doors. He confirmed that the locks could have been picked without ruining them. This meant that, while her story about the stalker might be a fantasy, the apartment could have been broken into without leaving evidence.

The insurance company still balked at the valuation of the "magic" gemstones. They were not going to concede on this fact, of course, and I wasn't about to argue that they should. However, not knowing the law, she had failed to include all the associated costs in her statement. She had spent years hunting for these gemstones in the mountains. Factoring in the time and expense that went into acquiring them actually made them even more valuable than she had claimed. She'd had to pay for travel, lodging, and other expenses to collect those gemstones.

I approached the insurance company with an itemized list of acquisition costs. You say they're not magic? Okay, but there's nothing supernatural about her hotel bills and gas receipts, so let's talk about those mundane expenses. The insurance company pays for acquisition costs for all my commercial clients—why not for her gemstones, magical or otherwise?

In the end the insurance company offered a settlement that she would never have been able to negotiate on her own without a full understanding of insurance law. She didn't know she could claim acquisition costs—and the insurance company's adjusters certainly weren't going to tell her. This was itself a form of fraud—fraud by omission of information. She was a vulnerable person being taken advantage of by a company that believed they could pull one over on her. But they couldn't do that once she had hired a professional for help.

HOW TO PROTECT YOURSELF

Fraud is real. And I certainly don't mean to suggest otherwise. Real fraud is bad and costs both the insurance companies and policyholders money through fake claims and the result of higher premiums. Real fraud should be fully punished under the law. However, cases of actual fraud are a tiny fraction of the legitimate claims filed every day. The vast majority of claims are legitimate losses resulting from hurricanes, tornadoes, hailstorms, fires, burglaries, car accidents, and other perils. The paranoia surrounding insurance fraud isn't justified.

Don't get caught in the nets being cast by hypervigilant or overzealous fraud detection departments. To protect yourself, hire an attorney at the first sign of trouble. Get an attorney if you suspect you are under investigation. Find an attorney if you have a legitimate claim denied on the basis of fraud or lack of evidence. Don't submit to examination or make a statement under oath without legal representation. If the insurance company is scrutinizing your claim or your good word, you already need professional help.

CHAPTER 4

A CULTURE OF BAD PRACTICES

IN THE MID-NINETIES my friend and fellow attorney Todd Hindin heard about a case where a State Farm office in Los Angeles discriminated against claimants with Jewish lawyers and claimants who had foreign-sounding names. Todd had a case against State Farm where his client, Singh, was being accused of staging an automobile accident to collect uninsured motorist benefits. Singh had a foreign-sounding name. Todd was his lawyer and also Jewish. He wondered if this was the reason State Farm had singled out Singh.

What he ultimately found was shocking. Certain State Farm offices, including the one that made allegations against Singh, had figured out that some subset of claimants committing fraud were being represented by Jewish attorneys. To better detect fraud, they started investigating all claimants represented by lawyers who were black, Hispanic, or Jewish, as well as those with a foreign-sounding name. The claims department memo on the matter became known as the "Jewish lawyers list." If the claimant was represented by an attorney on the list, the claim was sent straight to the fraud department for investigation. State Farm also had a similar memo directing that any claimants who were black, Hispanic, or Jewish or had a foreign-sounding name have their claim sent to the fraud unit as well.

These policies amounted to profiling. They were blatantly discriminatory and illegal. They were clearly a bad idea, but the claims department in State Farm's Westlake office in Los Angeles was more focused on finding fraud than acting ethically. This practice also had the added benefit of reducing paid claims. Lots of these claims were legitimate, but not all of them were pursued further. Some policyholders will drop small claims if they get denied or lead to an investigation. The claim isn't worth the hassle of being investigated or hiring an attorney.

> **Todd now had his hands on memos instructing claims adjusters to discriminate based on race, religion, and national origin when evaluating claims for possible fraud.**

Suspecting bad faith on the part of the insurance company, Todd subpoenaed State Farm for records showing how the company processed claims and launched investigations. A judge ordered State Farm to release the documents. Todd now had his hands on memos instructing claims adjusters to discriminate based on race, religion, and national origin when evaluating claims for possible fraud.

These documents were hard proof that the claims department, at least at this one State Farm office, was operating in bad faith. They had created a culture focused on underpaying claims. Claims managers and adjusters were compensated and graded based on their ability to pay less on claims. Claims adjusters that paid out the least in claims were rewarded, and so were their managers. The claims department was rewarding employees for underpaying customers rather than paying claims fully and properly.

Todd shared these documents with other attorneys, me included, so that we could use them in our own cases. This was not an isolated incident. We all had cases like these. While I am not Jewish, I had Jewish clients. I represented black, brown, and immigrant clients as well. Many of them were also having their claims sent to the fraud department for no reason other than the color of their skin.

Todd eventually settled the case, which had involved a $35,000 claim, for $30 million. State Farm settled confidentially to avoid embarrassment and further legal actions. The settlement agreement stipulated that Todd return company documents to State Farm, which he did. However, he had already handed out copies to others. When State Farm learned about these copies, which were being used in other cases, the company asked the judge to order Todd to return these copies as well. The judge refused since the original settlement said nothing about returning copies.

State Farm was concerned about the documents because they could be used in other lawsuits, which they were. We used them at our firm. So did other attorneys. The documents clearly showed the company's bad faith practices and toxic culture. They were embarrassing and terrible for public relations. These practices were at odds with the family-friendly and community-focused image that the company wanted to project. "Like a good neighbor, State Farm is there" has been the company's slogan for so long that everyone knows the jingle. But these practices initiated in the Westlake claims office betrayed that image. There was nothing friendly about the business culture of State Farm claims departments.

Now, the best way to handle such a situation would have been to not engage in bad faith practices. Failing that, once the damage was already done, the company could have handled the situation better by issuing a public apology, reforming the company culture, and moving on. But that's not what State Farm did. Instead they hit back against Todd. They hired a private detective to track down Singh, the original plaintiff in the case, and produced a recording that allegedly captured Singh admitting to fraud. With this recording in hand, State Farm sent their general counsel to Washington, DC, to ask the attorney general to prosecute Todd. State Farm also sued Todd in order to get back the $30 million settlement money.

This lawsuit was illegitimate. First of all, the tape didn't prove fraud. There was no such admission on the recording. Second, the issue of fraud had already been litigated and settled. The case was now what the legal community calls *res judicata*, which is a matter that has already been resolved in court and cannot be pursued again by the same parties. Rulings *can* be appealed, of course, but you cannot launch a new lawsuit for a settled matter.

That didn't stop State Farm from lodging the lawsuit anyway. Todd countersued their entire board of directors. The lawsuit against Todd was eventually dismissed but not without creating many headaches. A judge froze Todd's assets the week before his daughter was getting married, which meant he couldn't pay vendors for the wedding. The lawsuit was also a public relations blunder for State Farm. An embarrassing matter that had already been settled quietly was brought back into active litigation and once again put under public scrutiny. The Jewish lawyers list ended up back in the news and became part of a published decision.

BLAME THE COMPANY CULTURE

The most shocking thing about this story is that State Farm had distributed the Jewish lawyers list openly within the company. This was not some *isolated* practice but an actual policy that had gone through official claims management at its Westlake office. One wonders how such a thing could happen at such a large company with so much to lose. This kind of egregious discrimination was unacceptable. One also wonders how a company develops a culture so toxic that such a practice could be adopted without causing pushback from within the company.

These people probably did not consider themselves racist, but they were enacting and carrying out discriminatory policies in order to cut claims payments. This is a testament to the business culture of the claims department. These policies were likely intended, at least originally, to curb fraud. They also would help claims adjusters meet what State Farm used to call "severity goals," which were benchmarks set by the company that encouraged adjusters to pay out less in claims.

Documents from State Farm showed that these incentives went all the way up the ranks. The claims managers also received bonuses when their teams reduced what they paid in claims. The managers' superiors applied pressure and received pressure. This created a claims department culture geared toward underpaying claims rather than paying them accurately and fully. Referring cases to the fraud department without any evidence of wrongdoing by targeting individuals based on race and religion was just another method of hitting those severity goals.

> **The job of an adjuster should be to pay the right amount promptly, not the lowest possible amount.**

This practice is not right. The job of an adjuster should be to pay the *right* amount promptly, not the lowest possible amount.

The fact that no one from the claims or fraud department spoke out publicly or apologized gives insight into the company culture. The fraud department was focused on rooting out fraud no matter the method used. The claims department was happy to send claims out for investigation rather than pay them. No one spoke out because there was no incentive to do so. In fact, all the incentives encouraged them to continue the discriminatory practices. The employees may not have liked the policies, but their jobs and careers depended upon doing the wrong thing.

It's easy to look down at people for not speaking out, but an entrenched bad faith culture normalizes practices such as these. The entire company culture is geared toward getting employees to act in a certain way. Claims adjusters were expected to do the wrong thing. Speaking out would put their jobs, livelihoods, and reputation, to say nothing of bonuses and promotions, at risk. Rather than blame the adjusters, we should first and foremost blame the company culture and those responsible for instilling it.

We cannot depend on whistleblowers to prevent bad company cultures from taking root and becoming entrenched. People don't want to lose their livelihoods, so they will often do what has to be done to keep their jobs. Adjusters who actually do honest work and make sure that policyholders get paid don't stick around. They either get pushed out or passed over until they quit in frustration. When this happens, you're left only with the bad actors, and the bad faith culture becomes entrenched.

The only way to change the situation is to change the culture. Insurance companies have to do away with incentives that promote claims underpayment and delay. Lower-level employees cannot fix the problem. Insurance claims managers and executives need to foster a culture of good faith practices by incentivizing the claims department to pay claims accurately and promptly.

WHEN ARBITRATION ISN'T WORTH IT—AND THAT'S THE WHOLE POINT

The Jewish lawyers list was a blatant violation of good faith. Other bad faith policies, while just as egregious, aren't always as obvious. Innocuous small print seems unimportant until you file a claim. For example, arbitration clauses that limit how claims decisions may be disputed are now being written into policies. These clauses require disputes to be handled through arbitration at the insurance company's chosen venue, which is often not where the policy was sold or the loss occurred. Most policyholders don't find out about these "small-point" clauses until they have a claim denied and have to travel out of state to dispute the decision.

About ten years ago, a group of doctors at an eye-care center joined together to purchase an outdoor shopping mall in Melbourne, Florida, as an investment. This was a large facility, about twelve million square feet, that they converted into offices for call centers. Unfortunately the facilities suffered major damage during Hurricane Matthew in 2016. The wind tore a section of the roof, separated air-conditioning units from their brackets, and sent large metal plates skittering across the roofs. The flying debris poked holes through the roofing, letting water in. Everything was damaged—the walls and floors, the computers and servers, everything. Operations had to be shuttered while they cleaned the place up.

The property was insured through a surplus lines carrier, which is an insurance carrier that is not licensed in the state where the policy is sold. Surplus lines carriers can be used to obtain insurance coverage that may not be offered by carriers admitted in the state, which have to follow state regulations governing what they can cover and how much they can charge.

While some policyholders may purchase policies from surplus lines carriers, they do not realize that surplus lines carriers are able to skirt pro-consumer regulation because they aren't admitted carriers, meaning that they are not required to follow many insurance commission regulations. Many issue policies with arbitration clauses that often dictate which state's laws apply and may stipulate that arbitration be done elsewhere, even very far away, where the policyholder cannot easily and affordably travel.

The doctors who owned the call center ran afoul of this problem. The entire facility was extensively damaged, but the insurance company only wanted to pay for some of the damage. The insurance company claimed that the water damage in the other buildings was the result of old leaks. Though sold in Florida, a state with stronger consumer protections for policyholders, the policy required arbitration to occur in New York in accordance with New York law. Many insurance companies want arbitration to be done in New York because it is a state with laws that are friendly to the insurance industry. In Florida, where our clients had bought the policy, the insurance company would have had to pay our clients' legal fees if we won the case. In New York, there are no such protections.

What this meant was that in addition to the policyholders having to contend with travel costs and the inconvenience of contesting the claim in another part of the country, they lost valuable legal rights. If the arbitration didn't go well, they also couldn't file a lawsuit in Florida—according to the policy, it had to be filed in New York.

I first heard about the case from their general counsel, who did not have a law license in New York. I did, so he brought me in to help. I started by touring the facilities in Florida and meeting with the property manager and maintenance staff. No one from the insurance company had even bothered to talk to them before denying most of the claim. They showed me where the air conditioners had been pried away and where the debris had damaged the roofing. The damage was clearly fresh from the storm and not an old leak as the insurance company was claiming. One of the buildings even had a large skylight knocked out, which was never mentioned in the insurance company's report. There was no way they could have missed the skylight, nor was there any way that the punctures to the ceiling were preexisting. The damage was clearly from the hurricane.

There is often no effective recourse for policyholders when their claims are denied if arbitration must be done so far away. The cost of arbitration out of state can be prohibitively expensive. Legal

> **There is nothing to gain by going to arbitration, much less court, a thousand miles away and spending more than you could possibly win. The insurance companies know this.**

fees and travel costs can exceed the cost of the claim. That wasn't the case for the doctors with the call center, whose claim was for $7 million, an amount you don't just walk away from. But for most people, especially noncommercial policyholders, the fight isn't worth it. There is nothing to gain by going to arbitration, much less court, a thousand miles away and spending more than you could possibly win. The insurance companies know this, which is why they created the practice and hide it in the small print buried deep in the insurance policy forms. They know that out-of-state arbitration is difficult and expensive for the policyholder. They want the policyholder to walk away.

In such cases there is often no way to make the person whole through litigation. Many states have consumer protections that require the insurance company to pay legal costs if the insurance company is in the wrong, which encourages them to pay claims correctly in the first place. Unfortunately this is not the case in New York nor many of the other places where the insurance companies insist on doing arbitration.

When insurance companies have so much leverage and know they won't be challenged, they can get away with underpaying claims. They know many policyholders cannot afford to challenge the company. This is why it is so important for state legislatures and regulators to enact strong consumer protections for policyholders. The insurance company should have to pay legal fees when they wrongly deny a claim. No one should have to travel across the country from where the loss happened or where the policy was sold to seek justice. Requiring them to do so often means there is no way for the policyholder to be made whole after a loss.

Some states prohibit carriers from requiring arbitration to be handled out of state. We are actively lobbying in Texas and Florida, which have in-state protections but still allow arbitration to happen out of state, to change the law and require arbitration and litigation to take place where the policy is sold. Policyholders should be protected by the laws of the state where the policy is sold and where the loss occurs. But until appropriate consumer protections are enacted in all fifty states or at the national level, the insurance companies will keep trying to move arbitration to states that lack strong consumer protections.

FIGHTING BACK WITH CLASS ACTION LAWSUITS

Insurance companies have tremendous leverage over policyholders who cannot afford to fight back in court. Requiring policyholders to travel great distances for arbitration means that there is no effective way to dispute small claims. Going to court or arbitration out of state can cost more than the amount in dispute. There is no way for the policyholder to be made whole fighting these battles one case at a time. Fighting individual cases over small amounts is a losing proposition for the policyholder.

The best way for policyholders to level the playing field is to launch class action lawsuits. In a typical class action lawsuit, a plaintiff sues the defendant on behalf of a larger group with similar cases. Class action lawsuits can be launched on behalf of a large group of plaintiffs without them all having to be present or active in the lawsuit. In class action lawsuits, each policyholder might only have a little skin in

> **Class action lawsuits are often the only recourse for the average policyholder when small amounts are at stake.**

the game, not enough to be worth fighting one case at a time, but in the aggregate the amount of money can be a lot. This levels the playing field between policyholders and the insurance company, allows individual policyholders to be made whole, and can expose bad faith practices that might otherwise go unchallenged. Class action lawsuits are often the only recourse for the average policyholder when small amounts are at stake.

When I used to run marathons, running many miles a week, I would see a massage therapist, Doris, regularly at the local athletic club. She was a single mom, working hard to keep food on the table. She got into a car wreck that put her behind on bills. She had insurance through Allstate, which hadn't paid her for the full cost of the repairs. They repainted her car and put in new parts, but since the original paint was dinged up and many of the parts old, they charged her for the enhanced value of the car and subtracted the amount from her claim as "betterment." Allstate noted that her paint had already been worn out and that the carburetor was old before the repairs. Allstate argued that Doris was now better off than she would have been had there been no accident, and so they lowered her claim to reflect that fact.

"Are you sure that's what they did?" I asked, knowing that this was not a standard practice. "Because they can't do that."

She shrugged. "That's what they said."

I asked her to bring her paperwork to me. Upon reviewing her papers, I saw that she was right. They had deducted "betterment" from her claim. Nowhere in her insurance policy did it say that they were allowed to adjust the claim down for betterment, but they did so anyway. I assumed the adjuster did this thinking she wouldn't be able to fight back.

I made a call to her insurance company and talked to the adjuster. "Is this some kind of mistake?" I asked.

"No, no," he said. "We do this all the time."

"This is common practice?" I said. "You do this to everyone?"

"Absolutely, we do it every time."

"It's not just that she's a single mother and you're trying to take advantage of her?"

"No, we do this to everybody."

This may have been common practice, but it certainly wasn't legal. I had already reviewed her policy and knew that it said nothing about betterment. The repair was supposed to be paid in full minus a small deductible. The dispute was only for $425, but if this was Allstate's standard operating procedure, as they openly admitted, we had a class action lawsuit on our hands. I normally would not be able to take on such a small case. I would go broke trying to go after every small claim like that, which is what the insurance company was counting on. They wanted her to eat the cost quietly.

We filed a lawsuit in small claims court and started taking depositions. Both the adjuster and the claims managers openly admitted that this was standard operating procedure even though it wasn't allowed under the policy. I reached out to other attorneys who specialized in class action lawsuits. They agreed we had a good case, so we decided to work it together.

In the end, Doris's $425 dispute turned into a statewide class action lawsuit that resulted in a $25 million settlement. Doris wasn't owed that much money, of course. Almost all the settlement went to other policyholders. Allstate had been doing the same thing all across Florida. When you insure so many vehicles, a couple hundred dollars here and there adds up to millions. But again the insurance company has all the leverage. Most people do not think they can get an attorney or afford to go to court over a few hundred dollars, which allowed Allstate to take in millions of dollars in illegitimate profits.

Doris and all the other policyholders who had been cheated only got made whole thanks to the class action lawsuit. In fact, Doris, as the leader of the class action lawsuit, got her money and then some. The person who leads a class action lawsuit often gets paid a little extra for their role. She also didn't have to pay any attorney's fees out of pocket. That was a pretty expensive message for Allstate and likely had the company thinking twice before trying such shenanigans again.

This was a happy ending. The case was clear cut. Allstate had no right to deduct for betterment. We had paperwork showing exactly how much they had deducted for each customer. However, Doris could never have stopped this wrongful practice and taken them to court without us filing a class action lawsuit.

AN INDUSTRY-WIDE PROBLEM

In a competitive market, honest insurance companies cannot compete with those cheating their own customers.

The bad faith practices discussed in this chapter and throughout this book are not the doings of evil people. Rather, they are the creation of a bad business culture. Insurance companies have two major problems that create this culture. The first is unreasonable paranoia over fraud prevention that treats innocent customers like criminals. The second is an intense focus on claims savings that results in claims departments being pressured to shortchange the company's own customers. Once this culture takes root, overzealous fraud prevention or claims expense reduction may become a mere justification for the claims department to deny, delay, and underpay legitimate claims. The claims savings become the whole point.

This is an industry-wide problem that needs an industry-wide solution. Large insurers are under tremendous pressure to keep premiums down by underpaying claims. In a competitive market, honest insurance companies cannot compete with those cheating their own customers. When one company cheats their customers, the others are faced with a decision to follow suit in order to stay competitive. While unethical, these practices do cut costs and raise profits. State Farm was cutting costs through discrimination. The next insurer we discussed was cutting costs by making it difficult for policyholders to have their day in court and using small print to take away consumer protections. Allstate was cutting costs by subtracting "betterment" from claims even though it wasn't allowed. Insurance companies employ unethical practices because they are effective at cutting claims costs.

One not-so-silver lining of cost cutting is that while it keeps premiums down, policyholders often don't receive the coverage they thought they had and were paying for. They think they are fully covered with a good deal only to find out, upon having a claim denied or

Cheap insurance is cheap for a reason.

underpaid, that they didn't have the coverage they thought. Only at the point of having a claim denied do they realize that their insurance policy was truly "cheap" and wasn't as good as they thought—or their insurance carrier as reputable paying claims versus giving a cut-rate premium as they first believed.

If the claims adjusters were allowed to do their jobs correctly and assess claims accurately, premiums *would* go up. This is not a bad thing. Premiums need to be high enough to cover all legitimate claims. Cheap insurance is cheap for a reason. Unfortunately you get what you pay for—or rather you *don't* get what you *don't* pay for. Lower premiums are great, but not if they mean that the coverage isn't real. A better system would assess claims fairly and charge appropriate premiums.

HOW TO PROTECT YOURSELF

Reforming the entire insurance industry is the only real solution to these problems. The insurance claims culture has to change, which will require better legislation and regulation. We are lobbying hard for consumer protections that force insurance companies to assess claims accurately. While waiting for those protections, litigation and class action lawsuits that allow the little guy to stand up to insurance companies are important to help policyholders get paid what they deserve.

Reform will not happen overnight. Our law firm has been working on this for over thirty years. Other consumer advocates have been working at it even longer. In the meantime, you need to do all you can to protect yourself.

First, stop shopping for insurance solely based on price. Research carriers and the policies they often sell before buying. Remember that cheap insurance is cheap for a reason. Research the company and try to understand if the policy is different before buying. Be aware of the tricks that claims departments use to underpay claims and discourage challenges from policyholders. Avoid companies that have a reputation for employing these tactics.

Second, make use of the resources and tools that are freely available to learn more about your policy, your carrier, and your claims. The internet is a wonderful tool for learning more about individual companies and the industry as a whole. Don't believe the insurance companies' own reviews. They curate reviews and only showcase the happy customers. Read reviews on third-party sites. Consult industry experts and ask insurance agents about the insurer's reputation when it comes to paying claims. This book is a great primer on the topic. Our blog (www.propertyinsurancecoveragelaw.com) is another great resource for learning more about these issues and is fully searchable.

Third, have the right people on your side. Your insurance agent can also be helpful when dealing with the claims department. The bad faith culture is often specific to an insurer's claims department. A good insurance agent can help ensure that adjusters and their preferred vendors do their jobs right. While the claims adjusters are working to keep your claim down, a professional agent wants to keep you as a customer.

You should also have your own expert or engineer overseeing or reviewing repairs. Many insurance companies insist that repairs be done by their "preferred vendors," who complete repairs according to the insurance company's specifications. The claims adjusters often instruct them to do repairs the cheap way rather than the right way. For example, a good paint job can cover up shoddy repair work, especially to the untrained eye, so get a trained eye to take a look. Have your own architect, engineer, or other specialist assess damages and repairs.

This is especially important for large claims. Major construction work should involve your own engineer or architect. You want input from your own advocate, someone who understands the necessary repairs and thus won't let a bandage be placed over a major problem that will inevitably cost you more in the long run. There needs to be someone representing you rather than just the insurance company's interests during major repairs.

As long as the culture of bad faith practices exists, you have to be skeptical of what the engineers put into their reports, how insurance adjusters evaluate the claim, and how the vendors do the work. Have a good lawyer on hand to review situations that seem fishy, such as underpaid claims or suspicious charges. Get a lawyer when it makes sense, but in the current environment, you sometimes have to first be your own best advocate.

CHAPTER 5

YOUR INSURANCE COMPANY'S RELATIONSHIP WITH YOUR POLITICIANS

IN THE 1990s several auto insurance policyholders brought a class action lawsuit against State Farm, the nation's largest auto insurer, for repairing cars with aftermarket car parts instead of the manufacturer's recommended original parts. Insurance companies often treat aftermarket parts as if they are interchangeable with regular parts. I have heard insurance representatives say they are as good, if not *better than*, the genuine parts from the original manufacturer.

This is simply not true.

First, aftermarket parts are usually made overseas in countries that don't always have the best quality control, such as China. Sometimes these parts are fine and completely interchangeable. Often they are not. Edmunds, regarded as one of the best resources for automobile information, advises consumers to be wary of aftermarket parts. They don't always fit correctly and sometimes compromise crumple zones, making them potentially dangerous if you get in an accident. They may be prone to failure due to poor quality control. This isn't limited to auto parts either. In 2004 we represented homeowners and businesses in Florida where the cheap Chinese drywall started to fall apart shortly after being installed.

Second, even when aftermarket parts are identical to the official manufacturer parts, they may still lower the value of the property. Unofficial parts detract from the value of a car. No one wants to buy a Ferrari or Mustang—or even a Toyota Corolla—with an off-brand, knockoff engine. They want the parts made or recommended by the original manufacturer.

The lawsuit brought against State Farm turned into a nationwide class action lawsuit involving nearly five million policyholders who had received aftermarket parts. In 1999 an Illinois state court jury awarded the policyholders $456 million. The trial judge tacked on another $730 million in damages on a fraud claim, bringing the total judgment to more than a billion dollars.

This was serious money, even for a giant insurance company. State Farm appealed the lawsuit to the Illinois Supreme Court. In order to change the ruling, State Farm believed it would have to change the makeup of judges on the court—and, as crazy as it may sound, that is exactly what they set out to do.

They were not alone. The rest of the insurance industry, while not part of the lawsuit, also had a dog in the fight. Other insurance companies were engaging in similar practices. Many used aftermarket parts to cut costs at the consumers' expense, and they didn't want to stop. Much of the insurance industry rallied behind a Republican judge, Lloyd A. Karmeier, who was running for the swing spot on the Illinois Supreme Court. Insurance companies funneled money into

Karmeier's campaign and helped him win election in 2004, tipping the balance of the Illinois Supreme Court in State Farm's favor.

Not surprisingly, the court threw out the $1 billion judgment against State Farm the very next year. Some legal observers believed that Karmeier should have excused himself from the case, given the support he'd received from State Farm and the insurance industry. He did not. His swing vote essentially prevented the class action members from collecting their billion-dollar judgment.

Litigation didn't end there, however. In 2009, in a different case, the US Supreme Court ruled that elected judges must sometimes excuse themselves from cases involving major campaign contributors. This ruling set a new precedent that the plaintiffs in the original case against State Farm cited in a new appeal. State Farm had spent over $3.5 million on getting Karmeier elected. It appeared the insurance industry, and State Farm specifically, had "bought" a judge in order to get the decision overturned. The original class action plaintiffs launched a whole new lawsuit in federal court, now accusing State Farm of engaging in racketeering by working to influence a judicial election specifically to overturn a decision.

It appeared the insurance industry, and State Farm specifically, had "bought" a judge in order to get the decision overturned.

State Farm was now staring down a double barrel—not only could the billion-dollar ruling be reinstated, but perhaps as much as $8 billion in penalties and damages could potentially be added due to the racketeering allegations. This new case was set to go to trial in 2018. Karmeier himself was due to testify, which perhaps spooked State Farm. The company settled for $250 million to avoid what could potentially amount to billions of dollars in fines. The settlement closed twenty years of litigation, finally bringing some justice to over five million policyholders.

THE INSURANCE LOBBY VS. CONSUMER PROTECTIONS

This situation was the stuff of John Grisham novels, but this was not fiction. Nor was this an isolated event.

It will surprise no one that insurance companies sometimes cut corners with repairs. However, even I was shocked by the facts of this case. What is even *more* shocking—and alarming—is that the insurance industry seated their chosen judge on the bench. The $1 billion judgment was overturned. Were it not for the work of diligent lawyers and some extraordinarily dogged plaintiffs willing to pursue a case for decades, the policyholders would not have prevailed.

This situation was the stuff of John Grisham novels, but this was not fiction. Nor was this an isolated event. The sad truth is that the insurance industry regularly engages in this kind of manipulation of elections and elected officials. While these circumstances are dramatic, the insurance industry regularly uses its money from your premium dollars to influence the regulatory and legislative environment in more mundane ways every single day. Your elected officials and their appointees are closely tied to your insurance company and subject to the influence of legions of insurance industry propagandists. The insurance industry employs an army of lobbyists to influence politicians and policy in all kinds of ways.

The industry has no reservations about paying these lobbyists top dollar. By investing a few million dollars into a judicial election campaign, State Farm was able to see a $1 billion judgment against them overturned, at least temporarily, and what amounted to an over three-hundredfold return on their investment. You can't get returns like that anywhere else, and so insurance companies are happy to invest millions of dollars into lobbying for their agenda.

That would be fine if their agenda was pro-consumer, but it's not. The insurance industry is hell-bent on paying less in claims, the consumer be damned, and will lobby hard against laws that might hold it accountable for wrongdoing. The claims department is where the most dollars exit insurance companies, so cutting costs usually means paying customers less on claims. Now, a claim is either legitimate or not, and if it is legitimate it should be paid in full. No insurance company is *over*paying claims, and fraud is relatively uncommon, which means that major reductions in payouts generally mean that legitimate claims must go unpaid or underpaid.

When legitimate claims don't get paid, policyholders have to seek justice in the courts, which is expensive without consumer protections that make the insurance companies pay legal fees when they lose a case. So of course the insurance lobby is hard at work trying to prevent and do away with consumer protections that make it easier for policyholders to get the money they are owed. The result is that it is harder for policyholders to get justice.

Pointing fingers at State Farm is easy, but this is not a problem with just one company. Much of the insurance industry engages in the same practices, and the whole industry lobbies against laws and regulations that might hold them accountable for doing so. We cannot expect the insurance industry to fix the situation itself, nor can we expect individual insurers to step up and do better. They should, but they won't—and in a way they *can't*. Insurers are under tremendous competitive market pressure to reduce claims costs. Most policyholders shop for insurance based on price. Companies that underpay and cheat their own policyholders have lower costs and can charge lower premiums. When State Farm replaces original parts with cheap aftermarket parts from overseas, they are able to lower claims payments and then often lower premiums. Their competitors are then forced to do the same. This creates a race to the bottom. Insurance companies must choose between doing right by the consumer or staying in business. Most will take the low road every single time. Those that take the high road make less profits, or they market in a different manner to attract customers willing to pay a little more to obtain full claims payments.

This is why pro-consumer protections are so important. The insurance industry has historically proven that it cannot police itself. The only answer is to enact laws and regulations that protect consumers and empower them to seek justice in court.

Unfortunately the insurance industry is vehemently lobbying against such laws and regulations. They are buying the favor of politicians and regulators to ensure that the environment remains favorable to the insurance companies, not their customers, influencing not just the agenda of legislatures, courts, and bureaucracies but even their makeup.

PUTTING LIPSTICK ON A PIG: HOW THE INSURANCE LOBBY SPINS ITS ANTI-CONSUMER AGENDA

While insurance companies may be willing to buy off politicians and bureaucrats, the public doesn't take kindly to being hoodwinked by their elected officials and their appointees. Much of the legislation that the insurance industry lobbies for is anti-consumer. This is not a great look and betrays the pro-family, community-oriented image that insurance companies want to project. As a result, insurance lobbyists often dress up their agenda in a consumer-friendly disguise.

The insurance industry has learned to spin its anti-consumer agenda as the solution to real problems that consumers face. They are very good at propaganda, taking an issue with a kernel of truth and offering a solution that, while lowering costs, typically doesn't actually address the problem. They will often make the problem out to be much more dire or bigger than it actually is.

> **The insurance industry has learned to spin its anti-consumer agenda as the solution to real problems that consumers face.**

In a previous chapter, we looked at how "fraud prevention" can be used to slow and deny legitimate claims. This is a perfect example. Insurance fraud is real, though comparatively rare as compared to legitimate claims. The fraud prevention tactics that insurance companies employ often result in honest consumers having their claims delayed, denied, or underpaid. Insurance companies are able to pass these tactics off as pro-consumer, which they are not, by claiming that fraud drives up premiums. Fraud can drive up premiums, but the industry overstates the amount of fraud. Fraud is not having a major effect on premiums because insurance fraud isn't that common. But by pretending that it is and making up statistics, the insurance industry is able to enact "anti-fraud" measures that result in legitimate claims being denied.

Such misrepresentations allow the insurance company to lobby for anti-consumer legislation while minimizing the public and political backlash. Unfortunately this happens all the time.

Case in point: the insurance industry in Florida is currently waging a war against repair and restoration contractors that use assignment of benefits (AOB) contracts, which are contracts allowing policyholders to sign over the right to make claims and collect benefits to a third party. With an AOB in hand, a contractor can bill the insurance company under a policy and collect benefits without the policyholder's involvement.

This is not a new arrangement. Doctors and hospitals have been having patients sign AOBs as part of their standard paperwork for years. This is why you don't have to bill the insurance when you go to the doctor. Medical providers are able to bill insurance directly because you allow them to do so. You just sign the paperwork, fork over the co-pay, and the billing department takes care of the rest. It is easy to see why this appeals to policyholders. They don't have to deal with the insurance company at all.

The appeal of AOBs to policyholders making claims against homeowner or commercial insurance is the same—*convenience*. After suffering a loss, the policyholder wants to wave a magic wand that will make the problem go away. Policyholders just want someone to take care of the whole matter, do the repairs, and handle the entire billing process. AOBs allow them to off-load the entire process onto the contractor.

The problem is magic wands don't exist.

The problem is magic wands don't exist. Signing an AOB and trusting the contractor to do the work right can be a mistake. You are literally signing away many of your rights as a policyholder. There are many honest contractors who do good work. There are also bad contractors who don't do good work. Some contractors may try to use your policy to overcharge the insurance companies. If this happens and the insurance company refuses to pay, policyholders who have signed AOBs can find themselves a third party to a legal dispute over their own policy and their own property. Having signed over their rights, the policyholder may not be able to do much but sit and wait while the insurance company and the contractor try to resolve the issue.

Meanwhile, the work might go undone while the claim is in dispute. Some policyholders find themselves stuck in a state of limbo, unable to return home or reopen businesses while they wait for the insurance company to pay and the contractor to finish the work. The contractor blames the insurance company for not paying the claim. The insurance company blames the contractor for overcharging. They go to war, and the policyholder gets caught in the cross fire. The claim doesn't get paid. Quite often, the work doesn't get finished. When this happens, there is little the policyholder can do but sit and wait while the insurance company and the contractor work it out.

If the dispute turns into a lawsuit, the stalemate can drag on indefinitely. The policyholder is powerless to end the dispute, as they are now a third party and can neither sue nor settle. The insurance company won't even work with the policyholder, sometimes won't even talk to them, because for all intents and purposes, the claim doesn't belong to the policyholder. It belongs to the contractor with the AOB. There's no reason for the insurance company to negotiate with the policyholder when the contractor controls the policy. The dispute may drag on for days, weeks, months, years—and there may be little the policyholder can do.

Insurance companies in Florida, and elsewhere, cite all these problems when lobbying against AOBs. However, their real qualm with AOBs has nothing to do with the policyholder. They aren't concerned about the policyholder. They want to take away power from contractors who stand up against the insurance company's lowball tactics.

I attended a national insurance industry convention where Lisa Miller, a prominent insurance lobbyist and consultant, talked about AOBs. A former deputy insurance commissioner, Lisa now represents and advises many of the major insurance companies offering personal and commercial residential policies in Florida. I have known her for the last twenty-five years. She is bright, eloquent, and informed. With her being an insurance lobbyist and me running a firm that represents policyholders, we are often on opposing sides of the debate, which is exactly why I listen when she speaks on the insurance industry's legislative agenda.

Miller blamed AOBs for a slew of frivolous lawsuits launched against insurance companies by disreputable contractors. According to her research, which she shared with me after her talk, more than a quarter of first-party property insurance lawsuits in the state were brought by restoration contractors and roofers. She claimed that these contractors were using AOBs to file inflated claims to extract undue money from the carriers.

These lawsuits often cost the contractors nothing. Florida has strong consumer protections that require the insurance company to pay legal fees if they lose a lawsuit. These protections were designed to protect policyholders by empowering them to go to court over disputed amounts that are less than the legal costs. Florida's consumer protections prevent insurance companies from leveraging the cost of going to trial against policyholders whom they have wronged.

Policyholders are getting hit not only when a claim is disputed but also every month when they pay their premium.

Unfortunately, according to Miller, contractors were using consumer protections, along with AOBs, to do the very same thing to insurance companies. The cost of legal fees and the prospect of losing at trial have the insurance companies over a barrel. They end up settling lawsuits over claims that they may even consider frivolous or inflated in order to avoid trial. According to Miller, AOB abuse in Florida has resulted in an additional $1 billion in inflated claims and frivolous lawsuits in recent years. These costs get passed on to the consumer in the form of higher premiums. Policyholders are getting hit not only when a claim is disputed but also every month when they pay their premium.

There is, again, a kernel of truth to this narrative. The practice is real. There are bad contractors abusing AOBs to extort money from insurance companies. There is a whole cottage industry of law firms helping them game the system in this way. I know attorneys who have been severely sanctioned for this practice.

However, the insurance lobby is only telling half the story. They would have us believe that the fault in these lawsuits always lies with the contractors. But the reality is that for every dishonest lawsuit lodged by a shady contractor trying to get more money out of the insurance company, there are many more honest contractors doing good work who cannot get paid fairly. The construction business is not as full of crooks as the insurance lobbyists try to make them seem. Many reputable restoration contractors who have worked in the industry for decades have detailed the hassles they deal with when filing claims. I know because I have represented them.

None of this was an issue fifteen years ago, but as we saw in previous chapters, the entire culture of claims departments is increasingly focused on one goal: pay less in claims. The contractors are in the same position as policyholders—all too often the insurance company doesn't want to pay up when it should.

And that's the real reason insurance companies want to do away with AOBs. It has nothing to do with protecting the policyholder, the ostensible reason given by the insurance lobby, and everything to do with taking away any leverage from contractors trying to get paid. Without AOBs, contractors cannot easily take the insurance company to court if a claim is denied. The policyholder has to get involved with the dispute.

We need laws and regulations that ensure that reputable contractors get paid for doing a first-rate job. If contractors can't get paid in full, they won't do the job right. Cheap, low-quality work is easy to hide under a coat of paint or under the hood of a car, at least until it starts to fail. We should not be incentivizing contractors to do work on the cheap. Only the contractors cutting corners and breaking the law will be able to stay in business. This is bad for policyholders and the good contractors trying to make an honest living.

The insurance companies are demonizing contractors. They are pretending that a few bad apples are representative of the entire industry. They paint professional contractors who come in from out of state after a large-scale disaster as fly-by-night carpetbaggers coming in to prey on the community when this couldn't be further from the truth. This is unfair and almost slanderous. Contractors, whether local or coming in from out of state when disaster strikes, help restore and rebuild homes and communities. Restoration contractors who follow local building codes and use quality methods and materials are not the enemy. We should be thanking them for their hard work. They deserve to be paid for a job well done.

If insurance companies were truly interested in protecting policyholders, they wouldn't be lobbying against AOBs and consumer protections. They would be lobbying for stronger consumer protections that make sure that the policyholder gets the work done and the contractor gets paid. But that isn't what they want. The insurance industry just wants total control of the process so that they get to decide how work is done and what is to be paid without criticism or penalty.

The insurance industry has refused to even compromise on the matter. Sean Shaw, formerly an attorney at our law firm, was a representative in the Florida state legislature, where he worked on a bill that would have required contractors to finish the work before an AOB could be enforceable. We believed this was a good compromise that would ensure the work got done without leaving the policyholder hanging. If the contractor was asking too much, the insurance company could still take them to court, but the policyholder wouldn't get caught in the cross fire.

The insurance lobby was not interested in the compromise. They wanted to prevent contractors from being able to use AOBs at all because the AOBs allowed them to take advantage of Florida's strong consumer protections. The insurance companies don't want to deal with professional contractors who know how the repairs should be done. They want to deal directly with policyholders so that they can cut costs by doing only the bare minimum, if even that. Shoddy work is easy to hide and often overlooked until years later when it has to get corrected.

Sean is no longer in the legislature. The battle between the insurance lobby and repair contractors in Florida is still going on since the insurance industry turned up its nose at a viable compromise that would have solved the policyholders' problem. The insurance lobby is still descending upon the capitol in Tallahassee and whipping policymakers into a frenzy over AOBs. Meanwhile, policyholders who cannot get their claims paid or their repairs finished are the powerless losers.

HOW TO PROTECT YOURSELF

The insurance lobby is connected, moneyed, and powerful. Insurance companies are gigantic corporations with plenty of cash to lobby for legislation that ultimately only protects them.

Much of the legislation regulating the industry is actually written by insurance lobbyists. In 2011 the *Herald-Tribune*, published by a major media group in Sarasota, Florida, reported that insurance lobbyists wrote a controversial bill that would prevent Citizens Property Insurance Corporation, the state-run carrier, from effectively competing with private insurance companies. The insurance industry literally wrote the bill. This is not an uncommon practice. Lobbyists often write bills that hit the floor of the legislature without any changes whatsoever. This happens in many states, not just Florida.

Unfortunately the policyholder has no comparable counterpart to the insurance lobby advocating for the interests of consumers. There *are* organizations advocating for policyholders. Amy Bach, a consumer advocate and attorney, cofounded United Policyholders in 1991, and they have been advocating for policyholders in all fifty states ever since. The Consumers Union, known for the *Consumer Reports* magazine, advocates for insurance policyholders. The Consumer Federation of America has a branch led by Robert Hunter, a former Texas commissioner of insurance, which also advocates for policyholders. But these nonprofits don't have anywhere near the same amount of money, and therefore political power, as the insurance lobby. For every Amy Bach or Robert Hunter fighting for policyholders, there are hundreds of industry lobbyists working against the interests of consumers. These insurance lobbyists have loads of industry money, and they are in bed with many of your policymakers, actively working against your interests.

Sometimes the lobbyists *are* your policymakers. In most states, the insurance commissioner is the head regulator of the industry. This position is often appointed by the governor and staffed by a revolving door of insurance industry insiders. While it makes sense to have someone who knows the industry overseeing regulations, we have "foxes guarding the henhouse." There's nothing wrong with being a fox, but you don't want them in charge of the henhouse. Insurance regulators should be consumer advocates, not industry advocates , because it is a conflict of interest to have industry people overseeing watchdog agencies and acting as regulators. After leaving office, these insiders usually go back to work in the insurance industry. Many regulators thus have a strong incentive to watch out for the insurance companies that will be paying their salaries when they leave office.

I attended a Texas Association of Public Insurance Adjusters conference with my colleague Rene Sigman where we had to sit through a talk given by Todd Hunter, a state legislator representing a district in Corpus Christi. Hunter talked about his constituents being harmed by bad faith insurance companies and the laws that failed to hold them accountable. Rene and I couldn't believe our ears. It was like we had entered a twilight zone. This was the same man who oversaw TWIA, the state-run insurer of last resort, as part of the House Insurance Committee while TWIA was severely underpaying policyholders following Hurricane Ike. TWIA committed numerous acts that potentially rose to the level of fraud in order to reduce claim payments under Hunter's watch. An insurance company attorney who has represented clients in the industry for some forty years, Hunter protected TWIA throughout all this and later, in 2011, helped pass legislation making it harder for policyholders to collect their claims in full. He has a long history of voting against the interests of policyholders. As recently as 2017, he voted for legislation that hurt policyholders along the Texas coast who were fighting with insurers that wouldn't pay their claims.

Rene stood up and set the record straight about how, despite claiming to now advocate for policyholders following Hurricane Harvey, he routinely voted against policyholders for over a decade and worked hard to protect insurance companies engaging in bad faith practices. The media also picked up on the story, and there have been multiple articles questioning where his loyalties really lie.

This is the best way to fight the insurance lobby. Individual policyholders cannot go it alone in this fight. We must band together and expose the wrongdoing of insurance companies engaging in bad faith practices, as well as the policymakers they have in their pockets. Policyholders need to speak up when they are being wronged and take their stories to court and to the media. We need to stand together, lock arms, and protest companies engaging in these practices.

Unfortunately this takes time and effort that many hardworking people simply do not have. Many people cannot fight back because they lack the time and financial resources. But there's no other way to stand up against the insurance lobby. Policyholders are being harmed by bad legislation being written by lobbyists.

While there aren't enough consumer advocacy groups, there are lots of great attorneys working hard to represent and protect policyholders. Our law firm fights for policyholders, and not just in the courtroom but also at state capitols in all the states in which we operate. I don't like going to capitols to talk to politicians and regulators—watching legislators work on legislation is like watching sausage being made—but consumers need advocates. At times it can feel like being David fighting Goliath. They have more money and power, but we are on the right side—and sometimes we win.

CHAPTER 6

WHEN THE INSURANCE ADJUSTER IS YOU

IN 2018 A RETIRED COUPLE, Jim and Joy Piburn, came to our Denver offices after suffering a major residential fire that burned their entire house to the ground. They lost practically everything in the fire. The silver lining—or what *should* have been the silver lining—was that the house and its contents were covered under a comprehensive homeowners insurance policy, as well as $20,000 of supplemental coverage.

I say that this *should* have been a silver lining because the insurance company did not make it easy for them to collect all they were due. State Farm had paid the claim made under their primary policy, though only after a lengthy delay while the policyholders performed a thorough item-by-item inventory of the losses. However, State Farm totally refused to pay the claim made on the supplemental coverage.

Performing that thorough line-by-line inventory list was not easy for Jim and Joy. The insurance company gave them a thick stack of forms to fill out. The insurance adjuster demanded a mountain of information about their contents. Not only did they want to know *what* was lost, they also wanted to know *where* and *when* everything was purchased. They requested model numbers and serial numbers. They wanted receipts and documentation of purchases. The insurance company wanted to know both the purchase price of each item and its current cash value so that they could pay the lower of the two figures. This required the couple to calculate the depreciation of mundane household items like dress shoes, laptop computers, kitchen appliances, furniture, lawn-maintenance equipment, and every other thing they had owned.

The Piburns hardly knew where to even begin, which isn't surprising, as they were not professional adjusters. They were just homeowners trying to get their claim paid after their house totally burned down. They struggled to remember everything they had purchased years ago. Many of the photographs, receipts, and other documentation had been destroyed in the fire. The insurance company was requesting information they didn't even have. They were actually told to return to the house, nothing but rubble now, and start digging through the fire debris full of dangerous toxins and carcinogenic material to see what they could find!

THE AMATEUR INSURANCE ADJUSTER

The problem here should be obvious: rather than sending out professional claims adjusters to do the job—*their* job—of taking inventory of the losses and calculating the value and any depreciation, a complex process that must be done in accordance with relevant laws and regulations, the insurance company outsourced the work to its own customers. Insurance adjusters failing to fully investigate claims, establish the facts of a loss, and evaluate all the benefits owed has become somewhat common practice in the insurance industry. This practice causes significant delays in getting claims paid by turning insurance policies into "self-serve" products.

Making insurance policies into self-serve products is done at the policyholder's expense. I am reminded of how, when I was a child, a gallon of gas cost about two quarters, and you didn't have to pump it yourself. Gas stations were "full service" back then. You would pull up and tell the attendant how much gas you wanted, and they would pump it while you sat in the car or got out to stretch your legs. Eventually gas stations realized that they could save money by having you pump your own gas. Today there are virtually no full-service gas stations outside of New Jersey, where state law bars you from pumping your own gas. In every other state, you now have to pump your own gas. Rarely can you find any full-service stations anywhere else. There can't be. The price of paying attendants would make the gas more expensive. Full-service stations can't compete with self-service stations.

> **Making insurance policies into self-serve products is done at the policyholder's expense.**

A similar situation is now at work in the insurance industry regarding some of these practices, including having policyholders doing the work the insurance company is obligated to do. The insurance company used to send professional adjusters out to assess all losses after a claim. After a fire, insurance adjusters would show up and assess the damage. They would look at the structure and contents and work with the policyholder to take stock of what had been destroyed. After water damage, they would check for mold and moisture in hidden places. They would then assist the policyholder in calculating the value of all losses and explain all benefits the policy afforded.

Today many insurance companies often ask the policyholder to do much of this work when filing a claim. While people don't mind pumping their own gas, especially if it will save them a few bucks, processing a complex insurance claim is not as straightforward and easy as working a gas pump. Policyholders are not experts at understanding the benefits and valuation clauses within insurance policies. Filling out the complex forms is time consuming. Calculating depreciation of property requires understanding of relevant laws and regulations. Indeed, depreciation is a confusing and nebulous concept for many claims adjusters, who often get it wrong. Laypeople might as well just be guessing at what they put down on forms. They don't know how to calculate the value according to industry standards and laws and were never warned that the insurance policy would require them to be an insurance expert if they suffered a catastrophe.

As with the vast majority of policyholders, the Piburns were not equipped to do this kind of work. They struggled to remember everything that they had lost in the fire. Without receipts and other documentation, which had burned up in the fire, they found themselves combing through fire debris to take stock of their losses. This is a dangerous activity that no one should be doing without the right training and safety gear. Even knowing what they lost, they didn't know how to value it properly. Not being claims adjusters, they didn't know how to accurately depreciate property to find the current cash value of items purchased years or decades ago.

The whole task was impossible, and the couple found themselves frustrated by a stack of forms that they did not know how to fill out properly. At times they wanted to just give up—and *that* was the entire point. The insurance company knew the process was hard and beyond their abilities. They were hoping that the couple would just give up and settle for less than they were actually owed.

Don't kid yourself. Big insurance companies could fill out these forms and assess losses on their own. Large insurance companies process thousands of claims per day. They know what things cost and how much use and condition lowers value. Much of the work they ask policyholders to do when filing a claim could be standardized, automated, and completed quickly by the insurance company. Some of the information they ask for isn't even necessary to process a claim. The rest they could collect and process more quickly and efficiently. The insurance company could also pay a significant undisputed amount quickly to soften the financial blow caused by a catastrophic loss.

The operative word here is *could*. They *could* handle this work for the policyholder, but they often do not. There is often no incentive for them to pay adjusters to take the time to accurately assess losses. Most people do not buy enough coverage for the contents of their homes. They either underestimate replacement costs or simply take solace in the fact their house probably won't burn down, blow away, or wash away in a flood. When an underinsured policyholder does suffer a catastrophic loss, there is little monetary incentive for the insurance company to pay professional adjusters to assess the claim accurately. From a strictly monetary perspective, the insurance company has no reason to pay adjusters to get an accurate assessment of such losses when they will have to pay out the full value of the policy up to its limits anyway. They can save on expenses by having the policyholder do all the legwork.

But that's only half the story. The insurance companies aren't just hoping to save on expenses by having the policyholders do the work. They are also hoping to save on how much they pay out in claims. They want you to do the work of assessing losses because they know how difficult this is for policyholders to do correctly. In fact, they intentionally make it more difficult. The process is designed to be rigid and time consuming. They want to frustrate the policyholder. When policyholders have a hard time assessing a loss, they are likely to give up, make mistakes, or underreport the amount of the loss.

You can be sure that if you overestimate losses, the insurance company will correct the record or even allege fraud on your part. But they aren't going to object if your claim is for less than you are owed. Though counterintuitive, policyholders are much more likely to underreport the value of losses in their own claims than they are to claim more than they are due.

Many honest policyholders would rather underreport their losses than risk claiming too much. People are afraid of inadvertently committing fraud.

In order to claim a loss, you have to know what was lost and how much it was worth. When a catastrophic flood, fire, or other disaster takes out the whole structure, policyholders often cannot remember everything they owned. They are also likely to underestimate—or at least underreport—the value of much of their property. The value of used cars can be looked up in the Kelley Blue Book. But what about everything else? How much is the matching bedroom set handed down in the family for four generations worth? What is the value of a ten-year-old mattress that is as firm as the day it was made? How much do you subtract from the value of a sofa that has cat-claw marks? What is the cash value of an attic full of Christmas ornaments that were purchased over the course of many seasons and even generations? What would it cost for a business owner to completely rebuild an office he or she has owned for decades?

Answering these questions is difficult for policyholders. Many honest policyholders would rather underreport their losses than risk claiming too much. People are afraid of inadvertently committing fraud. Many tend to give conservative estimates out of caution and ignorance about the cost of replacing older items with new ones. They may leave things off the report completely if they cannot find receipts or calculate the value of the property accurately.

This is especially true when filling out required forms, which can be rigid and difficult to do correctly. The paperwork is confusing, complex, and in many cases literally impossible to fill out accurately as requested. After struggling with difficult forms and a hard process that they should never have been asked to do, many policyholders may just give up, underreport the loss, settle for getting anything from the insurance company, and simply move on with their lives.

This is especially true when the insurance company delays the claim for months. Policyholders often need a claim paid quickly after catastrophic damage so that they can start restoration and repairs. Homeowners want to return home to their normal lives as soon as possible after a disaster. Likewise, business owners want to make repairs quickly so they can open back up for business without losing valued employees and customers.

The insurance companies understand the psychology of honest policyholders and will actually exploit this for their own advantage. Many are banking on policyholders getting frustrated and abandoning the claims process. If the insurance company would otherwise be paying the full claim value, there is little incentive not to see if the policyholders quit or undervalue their own claims out of frustration. In the worst-case scenario for the insurance company, it will delay paying the claim and save expenses by having its adjusters do less work. But often the policyholder comes back with an estimate that is even lower than what a professional adjuster would have reported.

We believe this is exactly what happened to the Piburns. They were given a lot of runaround and forms to fill out. They were asked to go digging through the debris to take an inventory of the loss. The claims payments were delayed for months. The insurance company had every financial incentive to see if they would walk away from the claim made under the supplemental insurance policy. State Farm was doing them no favors here. It certainly seemed like the company was forcing the couple to do all this work following a devastating and traumatic fire to save money. They certainly weren't making the process easy.

WHEN INSURANCE COMPANIES PUT YOUR HEALTH AT RISK

Taking an item-by-item inventory of their losses was not only difficult for the Piburns—it was dangerous and traumatizing. They couldn't remember everything they had lost. They had to search the debris for reminders and evidence of their losses. This should have been the job of professional insurance adjusters, but the insurance company had their own customers doing the work instead. The insurance company had a seventy-year-old woman literally digging through the rubble of her own life. This was emotionally taxing, even traumatizing. Just imagine finding charred picture frames with the photos burned to a black crisp behind the glass. It breaks your heart.

Digging through fire debris not only took a toll on their psychological health—it was also incredibly dangerous. A fire scene is inherently unsafe. Structure fires release all kinds of dangerous toxins and chemicals. Older buildings may still contain asbestos in the insulation and tiling. Many buildings still have lead paint. Asbestos and other fine particulate matter gets released into the air and stirred up again when disturbed. These particulates, when inhaled, can lead to scarring of the lungs, mesothelioma, and other ailments. Lead can cause cancer, developmental disabilities, and birth defects. And that's just the tip of the iceberg—there are all kinds of toxic chemicals that can be released when a house, regardless of age, goes up in flames. Even the fire retardant can be highly cancerous! Many of these toxins are absorbed directly through the skin.

Handling these materials and operating in such environments is a job for professionals, not the policyholder, and certainly not for an elderly retired couple. Professional adjusters have access to and training with the proper safety equipment for doing this kind of work. They use masks and latex gloves, even respirators and protective suits, as appropriate. Insurance companies have to follow Occupational Safety and Health Administration (OSHA) rules when sending their insurance adjusters into dangerous sites, but since the policyholder is not an employee, none of those rules apply. Policyholders may not even be warned about the dangers. They do not always have access to the safety equipment that professional adjusters are required to use.

Similar damages are not limited to the scene of fires. Earthquakes can leave buildings standing but structurally compromised and prone to collapse. Asbestos and other dangerous particulates can be shaken free. Flooding and water-damaged structures have their own set of dangers as well. Water is often contaminated with sewage that harbors dangerous bacteria. Indeed, snakes and alligators can be found lurking inside homes after a major flood. Water damage inherently leads to molds, many of which are toxic when inhaled. Mold can even be a problem after fires. When fires break out, firefighters will spray the structure down with water. The water can migrate throughout the building and settle in cavities, quickly leading to mold growth.

These dangers are not specific to homeowners insurance policies either. The same thing can happen with commercial buildings. Wherever there is fire, flooding, or any disaster that compromises the structure of a building, these dangers apply. Whether you are a

Whether you are a homeowner or a business owner, you are probably not a trained professional in handling hazardous debris.

homeowner or a business owner, you are probably not a trained professional in handling hazardous debris. Trained restoration professionals and insurance adjusters know how to work in these environments safely. Professionals have access to the right gear. They have the right training. They abide by industry guidelines and take the right precautions. But the average policyholder is not a trained professional. They don't always know how to be safe and should never be forced into a dangerous situation by their own insurance company.

Yet the insurance companies aren't always warning their own customers about these dangers. Insurance companies may even ignore or downplay the risks. Policyholders don't always know when their health is being compromised. Mold and lead poisoning can have subtle and nonspecific symptoms at first. Policyholders may not connect their headaches or lethargy to the conditions in which they are working or living.

This is unacceptable, sometimes even criminal. Policyholders should be warned of these dangers. They shouldn't be sent back into unsafe environments. They should not be asked to do dangerous work that should be left to the professionals. They shouldn't be doing work at all—they are the customers. Why are they processing their own claims when the insurance companies abandon their obligations?

Unfortunately, policyholders often don't know any better. When a giant insurance company tells you to dig through the rubble or sift through a water-soaked living room, you assume that this is the way it is always done. Policyholders don't always appreciate what the insurance company is putting them through. They don't always know when they are being asked to do a job that should really be done by professionals. They don't always know when their health is being put at risk. While insurance companies often state that the policyholder has to make a claim for a specific amount, most policyholders don't always know the full value of their claims. And they don't usually know that the insurance company has designed the process to be as difficult as possible in order to delay claims and lower the total amount that is paid.

People buy insurance to protect themselves. They don't expect the insurance company to put them in harm's way or to take advantage of them, but unfortunately that happens much more often than it should.

HOW TO PROTECT YOURSELF

The insurance company engages in these practices to save money on paying claims and avoid the expenses of investigational evaluation. It's not right, and it needs to stop. And while these things shouldn't happen, they often do. You cannot always rely on the insurance company to help you file your claim accurately or even to protect your health and well-being in the process. However, there are steps you can take to protect yourself.

First, policyholders need to understand that they did not buy a "self-service" insurance policy. You shouldn't be, to speak metaphorically, pumping your own gas here. You are not an insurance adjuster. A professional adjuster should be assessing your claim and calculating what you are owed for your loss—not you. Consider it a red flag if the insurance company is trying to get you to do the job of a professional adjuster. That is why you are paying them a premium every month. Demand that they do their job.

Second, understand that while the insurance company *should* explain what benefits you are entitled to under your policy, they may not. Read your policy to learn about the benefits and coverage to which you are entitled. Talk to your agent. Ask about exclusions and benefit limits so that you know what and how much is covered. If you have had a fire, ask about whether your policy will pay to remove old asbestos or lead paint. There is a good chance that your fire policy will cover both. But if you don't ask these questions, the insurance company may not bring up the issue. Know your benefits. Understand the cost of replacing lost or damaged property. Be sure that you are getting *all* of what you are entitled to under your policy.

Third, know the dangers of working at a site that has suffered water, fire, or other damages before entering. We have already discussed many of the dangers in this chapter. Further reading is available for free online at our blog and elsewhere. Do not let the insurance company put your health at risk. They may tell you to go out and take pictures after a disaster. Do not do so unless you know the risks and how to protect yourself. If the situation is dangerous, you should request a professional do the work. If the insurance company refuses, consider getting an attorney or other professional involved.

Finally, and this is important, understand that you may be owed *more* than the maximum dollar value stated in your policy. When the insurance company inappropriately delays or underpays your claim or puts your health at risk, they may be liable for damages and penalties. Many states have consumer protections that will not only get you the money you deserve under your policy but also award you damages for being mistreated or harmed.

In the case of the Piburns, we ultimately settled their initial dispute over a $20,000 policy for more than $1 million. Not only was the claim eventually paid, they were also compensated for having their payments delayed, their health placed in jeopardy, and their emotional well-being put at risk by the insurance company—and rightfully so. The insurance company's own adjusters should have assessed the damage. They should have cut them a check within a week. The couple should never have been exposed to such dangerous conditions, nor should they have had to do the job of the insurance company. They were entitled to compensation for what was a horrible and unnecessary ordeal that stretched on for over a year.

This was a happy resolution, but they had almost given up hope by the time they came to our offices. Their claim had already gone unpaid for a long time. No one would take them on as clients because the $20,000 supplemental claim did not seem like a big enough value to sue over. These cases can take a lot of time, work, and money to pursue. While there are attorneys who are passionate about protecting consumers, law firms would go broke pursuing every case over a smaller claim. Insurance companies are often able to get away with doing the consumer wrong when legal fees would exceed the disputed amount of the claim.

This is why it is important to understand that, at least in states with strong consumer protection laws, your claim may be worth more than you think. When the Piburns spoke with Larry Bache and Jon Bukowski, two attorneys in our Denver office, they recognized that the case was worth far more than the $20,000 they were owed under the supplemental policy. Colorado has strong consumer protections that penalize insurance companies for delaying claims. When your house or business burns down, having to wait many months or a year for your claim to be paid is unacceptable.

Further, we also knew that if the insurance company would

take advantage of an elderly retired couple, they would maybe do it to anyone. The insurer would only have saved a small amount on denying this one claim, but multiply that amount across the many claims handled every year and the insurance company could save millions. We did not, and do not, believe this case was an outlier. Many insurance companies engage in these kinds of bad faith practices. For many insurance companies, this kind of thing is standard operating procedure, enacted in a methodical and calculated manner to reduce expenses and raise profits.

When one company cheats, every company in the industry faces pressure to cheat in order to remain competitive. You cannot be a full-service gas station in a self-serve world. These are insurance industry–wide problems. Management consulting companies, such as McKinsey & Company and Accenture, instruct their insurance clients on how to save money. That's not to say that all insurance companies do these things all the time, but in order to compete, they are all under tremendous market pressure to lower costs at any expense, which often means at the policyholders' expense.

The insurance companies only get away with these bad practices because most people aren't insurance lawyers, and they don't know the law. They don't know about the consumer protections enacted to protect them. They don't know how claims are supposed to be processed. They don't know what the insurance company owes them under their policies.

To avoid being a victim of the insurance company, you have to educate yourself and remain wary. If something seems wrong, you may want to seek legal advice from those who do this for a living. You don't necessarily need to hire an attorney right away, but you might want to consider talking to one if something seems off. This is especially true if the insurance company isn't paying your claim. If you aren't happy or satisfied, call an attorney with experience handling the type of insurance claim problem you are dealing with. Many law firms in the business of representing only policyholders will be happy to listen to the outlines of your case to see if they might be able to help.

CHAPTER 7

DO BUSINESSES AND LARGE PROPERTY OWNERS NEED INSURANCE TO COVER THEIR INSURANCE?

WHEN HURRICANE IVAN struck Florida in 2004, Tops'l Beach Manor Condominiums suffered severe damage from the storm. The building sits right on the oceanfront near Destin, a prime resort area that draws tourists from all over. The beaches have sugar-white sand, and the water is crystal-clear blue. This was the beginning of high season, when snowbirds start coming down to enjoy the temperate fall weather, but many of the units could not be rented due to water and wind damage from the hurricane. The damage needed to be fixed fast, or they would have to start canceling reservations.

The building was insured by Citizens Property Insurance Corporation, the state-run insurer in Florida. The company wouldn't pay the claim until its experts completed an estimate. They sent several adjusters to survey the damage, but before they could finish their estimate, the insurance company sent them home to Texas, never to return.

> # They couldn't afford to do the repairs with the insurance company's offer. They also couldn't afford to keep letting the units go unrepaired.

Four months after the storm, a different set of adjusters was sent out to start the process from scratch. When they finally finished, the loss figure they determined was $2 million. The policy had a $1 million deductible, which meant that the owners would only receive a million dollars from the insurance company.

The board of directors for the condominium was shocked. This was nowhere near enough to do the repairs. The damage was severe. The storm had uplifted parts of the roof, allowing water to pour into various units. The exterior walls were damaged. The place was a mess. Moreover, being a mid-rise building, the construction crew would need a crane, which is not cheap, to repair the facades. A million dollars was not enough—neither was $2 million. They were being severely lowballed.

After six months of arguing back and forth with the insurance company while many of the units went unrented, the owners brought me into the case. They were between a rock and a hard place. They couldn't afford to do the repairs with the insurance company's offer. They also couldn't afford to keep letting the units go unrepaired. Meanwhile, the roof was still damaged and letting water in. They now had mold growing in some of the units.

I hired an independent expert to do another quick estimate. We needed a second opinion. After taking a look at the damage, he said it would cost at least $5 million, maybe $10 million, to repair.

Knowing this, I also reached out to the first set of adjusters that Citizens Property Insurance Corporation had fired. The head estimator told me that they had almost finished the estimate when the insurance company had pulled the cord. Their estimate was over $8 million and rising when the insurance company sent them home. That was more than four times what the second set of adjusters was estimating. This wasn't even in the same ballpark.

"You were almost done?" I asked. "How much would it cost to finish your estimate?"

"About fifteen thousand dollars."

I immediately put them on retainer and contracted them to finish the job. Their full estimate came to $12 million—or six times what the insurance company's second set of adjusting experts came up with. Factoring in the deductible, the insurance company was trying to get away with paying less than 10 percent of what was owed.

I took this information to Citizens Property Insurance Corporation and told them I knew what they were trying to accomplish. There was no denying what they had done. I had the original estimate from their own contractors. The insurance company hadn't liked that estimate, so they'd axed the contractors and selected someone else who would give them the figures they wanted.

THE DESELECTION PROCESS

This is what I call the "deselection process" of insurance experts. It is a now-common practice that insurance companies use to "shop" for experts and estimators who will give opinions to keep claims payment costs as low as possible. The insurance companies deselect engineers, vendors, estimators, accountants, and other experts who do not actively work to keep costs down for the insurance company by providing reports and opinions that support low claims payments. They don't want estimators who are accurate. They don't want engineers who recommend the correct repairs. They want experts who will keep the claim as low as possible by underestimating damage, finding loopholes and exclusions, and recommending cheaper restoration quick fixes that may or may not hold up over time.

Finding such "experts" has never been easier. The insurance companies select experts from pools of contractors, estimators, engineers, experts, and vendors competing against each other for business. These experts may be independent contractors, but they are hardly "independent" of the insurance company. They depend on the insurance companies for repeat business. They know they will lose work if they don't do what they think the insurance company wants. And they aren't wrong—they are very likely to be deselected for the next job if they aren't working to save the insurance company as much money as possible on the current job.

This creates a pool of experts, estimators, and vendors who are utterly dependent upon the insurance companies. Truly independent experts, estimators, and vendors get deselected or blacklisted. They aren't offered future work. Those left behind are in the insurance company's pocket.

While representing a corporate client that suffered losses during the collapse of a pier over the Delaware River, I had a confrontation with an engineer representing the insurance company. He had tried to appear nonbiased by claiming that only half of his work was from insurance companies. When asked how many projects he currently had active, he said 280.

"How many of those aren't from an insurance company or paid for by an insurance company?" I asked. "What are their names?"

He could only name a *single* case that didn't somehow involve the representation of an insurance company.

There is nothing wrong with working for an insurance company. But make no mistake: these are not "independent" vendors. Most are beholden to the insurance companies that provide substantial volume work. They go to insurance conferences. They schmooze with insurance industry executives to get more employment and projects to work on. They give "in-house" seminars to insurers. They are generally watching out for the insurance company that pays their bills, not policyholders. They know how to play the game to get repeat business. If they started estimating losses accurately and recommending appropriate repairs, they would get passed over for those that will provide opinions and findings supporting lower payments rather than honest assessments of loss and damage.

This isn't right. These experts and estimators are supposed to be independent and unbiased. When the insurance company sends experts to opine about the cause and extent of damages, most policyholders assume that they are unbiased. They assume that these people are giving honest estimates and recommending the proper repairs. In truth, the insurance companies aren't hiring the best experts returning the most accurate estimates. They hire those who come back with the numbers and recommendations that they think meet the insurance company's expectations. These experts are looking for ways to adjust your claim down to less than the fair amount owed by cutting corners with restoration.

The goal should be to accurately assess the loss and to perform a full and total repair, not to save the insurance company money by doing as little as possible.

Modern claims departments are under immense pressure from management to keep costs down. This is true of private insurance companies and even more so for public-private partnership companies, such as Florida-based Citizens Property Insurance Corporation and TWIA. Both of these entities have embarrassing records of handling claims poorly. Following Hurricane Ike, claims managers at TWIA were found to have fraudulently changed field estimates of damage without permission to lower claims payments.

Transparency and honesty are key.

Cheating customers is not the ethical way to cut costs. What Citizens Property Insurance Corporation did to Tops'l Beach Manor was wrong. Stopping an estimate because claims management dislikes high figures undermines the purpose of having insurance to cover losses. Estimates should be accurate assessments of what proper repairs will cost. If the estimate isn't accurate, the claim gets underpaid and the repairs cannot be accomplished in a proper manner. Of course, that is the whole point. Many insurance claims managers have created a business culture focused on paying as little as possible rather than paying claims fully and taking care of the customer.

The insurance company is within its rights to challenge and demand accuracy of the reports from estimators and experts. The manner in which they question and demand change needs to be transparent and in good faith. When insurance companies question a report or a filing by an expert, estimator, or other vendor, no financial pressure should be applied, and changes in draft reports should be explained to the policyholders. Transparency and honesty are key. The policyholder should be looped in about what is going on, not kept in the dark or told lies.

Citizens Property Insurance Corporation didn't do any of that, nor did they have good intentions. They didn't want an accurate estimate, and they deselected the original estimators to prevent an honest opinion from being completed. Ultimately, thanks to the work of our attorneys, the truth came out. The case settled for over $10 million, close to the same figure the original estimators had suggested. The insurance company could have saved themselves a lot of legal fees and a big hassle by simply paying what they already knew they owed.

THE TACTIC OF DELAY

While the policyholders eventually got their money, the whole process dragged on for months. Many units were empty through the high occupancy season while the owners waited for the insurance claim to be resolved so repairs could begin. Most policyholders count on prompt payment of insurance benefits following a catastrophe. Insurance claims proceeds are supposed to finance the repairs.

Policyholders often face two sets of losses after a hurricane: first, the direct cost of the storm damage reflected in repair and construction costs. Second, the economic loss resulting from lost revenue and temporary relocation. There is often no preventing the storm damage. But much of the lost business revenue can be prevented if the insurance company meets its obligations in a timely manner. In the case of Tops'l Beach Manor, the lost revenue of unrented units and the cost of relocation were not covered by the insurance policy despite these losses being the insurance company's fault. The delay in paying the claim made these losses worse, and controlling the situation was out of the hands of the owners. It was up to the insurance company—and it was taking its sweet time.

The bigger the claim, the more scrutiny it receives.

In today's insurance claims environment, businesses and homeowners simply cannot depend on insurance companies to pay promptly. This is especially true for commercial policyholders with claims that can reach into tens of millions of dollars or more. The bigger the claim, the more scrutiny it receives. On large claims, the insurance company will send out engineers, estimators, accountants, and insurance policy attorneys to nitpick every detail of the repair process in order to bring their claims payment costs down.

That kind of scrutiny takes time. Arguments over how to perform repairs, as well as the price to do so, can further delay repairs. Time is a luxury that business owners do not have when operations are disrupted. Lost revenue and damage to the business's reputation will continue to mount while operations stay disrupted. Businesses fail when they cannot satisfy customer demands. The doors have to stay open with orders filled, machines running, and operations active to bring in cash. Without cash flow, bills don't get paid, inventory doesn't get restocked, and payroll doesn't get met. Cash to a business is like blood to a human. Without insurance companies promptly producing benefits for quick repair and lost revenue, commercial business will die. Businesses hemorrhage money when they are down, and most cannot afford to be down for long, even on a temporary basis. Employees, customers, and clients will move on if you aren't back up and running quickly. Business owners need claims processed quickly.

Insurance companies can help take some of the pressure off by paying a partial estimate for a portion of the claim that is undisputed. This is not the full amount owed, but it does allow the policyholder to start repairs.

Unfortunately some insurance companies intentionally delay payment to extract concessions from the policyholder. They have leverage over you while your business is down. This can be used to convince the policyholder to accept less than they are owed. The partial estimate can be used to lowball the policyholder. The partial estimate often understates certain losses or suggests using cheaper materials, knowing that the policyholder may take less than they are owed if it means getting the money to start reconstruction now. With the business hemorrhaging money, it can be very tempting to just take the money as offered without stating objections to parties.

This is sometimes the rational choice, as you might lose even more if the claim is delayed further, perhaps going out of business entirely, but that doesn't make it right. The insurance company is abusing the situation.

Businesses buy insurance as a safety net. Commercial policyholders shouldn't be left wondering how they will make payroll, make repairs, or replace destroyed inventory after a loss when they bought and paid for insurance that is supposed to cover those risks. They shouldn't be left wondering where the money will come from. The money is supposed to come from the insurance company. Businesses buy insurance so that the money will be there to finance the reconstruction and weather the catastrophe immediately after disaster strikes, not weeks or months down the line.

INSURANCE FOR YOUR BUSINESS INSURANCE

No business owner wants to be caught in this situation. Unfortunately many insurance companies cannot be trusted to pay claims fully and quickly. Given this fact, business owners need to have "insurance" for their insurance. This is a sad comment on the insurance industry.

Today I advise prudent business owners to be prepared for the insurance company to fight, delay, and underpay claims—and they should have a plan B to get repairs financed right away so that construction can start and normal operations can resume. While insurance claim benefits are supposed to be this immediate safety net, business owners need to be able to finance the repairs on their own while waiting to collect from the insurance company.

Business owners should establish dedicated or agreed lines of credit so that in the event of a major loss, they can finance repairs right away. Businesses do not have to wait for the insurance company to pay the claim before starting repairs. In fact, businesses are obligated to the extent possible to mitigate further damage and loss after a disaster. For example, when a roof is leaking, you have a duty to at least temporarily repair the roof and stop the leaking so the situation does not get worse. After a major loss, the most important thing is getting the business running again before it fails. And the best way to do that is to start repairs immediately, whether or not the insurance company is meeting its obligation to pay you quickly and fully. The best way to do that is to have lines of credit already in place.

I have seen the difference establishing credit can make. Tops'l Beach Manor was not the only commercial property damaged during Hurricane Ivan. I also represented Edgewater Beach Owners' Association, which rents condominium units at the Edgewater Beach Resort located only a mile from Tops'l Beach Manor. Both buildings suffered similar damage during Hurricane Ivan.

Suzanne Harris was president of Edgewater Beach's board of directors. After Hurricane Opal in 1995, she learned firsthand the problems that can arise when the insurance company delays payment. She had been going back and forth with the insurance company about how the repairs should be done for a solid year before I started representing her in 1996. They were facing a problem with unrented units and lost revenue while they waited on the claim to be paid.

The insurance company wasn't paying for the repairs, so we went around them and financed the repairs through a bank. This allowed construction to finally start and gave the association breathing room while the case went to court. The case wasn't settled. There was no way she could have stayed in business without having done the repairs herself. The bank financing literally saved the business.

Thereafter, her bank had a contingent line of credit in place for disasters. When Hurricane Ivan was set to strike the area in 2004, Suzanne had lines of credit already established with the bank so that she could finance any repairs. She was not going to be caught unprepared.

In fact, she called me a few days before the storm for advice. She was considering paying Western Waterproofing, the company (now known as Western Specialty Contractors) that had done repairs after Hurricane Opal, to come to Destin in advance of the storm and stage their equipment in the shopping center parking lot across the street. This would cost the condominium association $30,000. It was a gamble. Meteorologists were not sure where the storm would make land. If the hurricane missed Destin, the association would be out the money. But if the building did sustain damage, the insurance company would cover the $30,000, and the association would have a construction crew ready to start repairs right away.

Hurricane Ivan looked to be a monster. If it did hit, there would be damage to buildings with oceanfront exposure. This was also the beginning of fall, and once again the winter rental season was about to start. About three quarters of the units were up for rent. They would lose a lot more than $30,000 in lost revenue if repairs weren't made right away. Once a hurricane comes through, finding restoration contractors becomes difficult. Everyone wants to hire them once they have damage. If Edgewater Beach didn't pay to book Western Waterproofing in advance, they might be waiting weeks or months just to find a construction crew.

"Could you wait the three weeks?" I asked.

"Three weeks could turn into three months."

"Well, then you don't have much choice," I said. "I'd take the chance on the thirty thousand dollars."

The association put up the money and brought in the crew. Sure enough, the hurricane landed in Pensacola, forty miles away, which put Destin on the stronger east side of the storm. Even without suffering a direct hit, the wind speeds were incredible. The building suffered a lot of damage. Fixtures were torn off the facades. The roof started to leak, and water poured down into the units. The damage from Hurricane Ivan was worse than from Hurricane Opal.

This time they had contractors ready to go. This time they had the money to pay them up front to get started. The construction crew was out picking up debris the very next day after the storm. The roof was patched quickly, and the building started drying out before the mold grew out of control. The building was fully restored within about three months. Because so many of their competitors were out of commission for much longer than Edgewater Beach Resort, business actually ticked up. The resort stayed fully booked throughout the whole high winter rental season.

This was only possible because Suzanne Harris had a line of credit ready and her own contractors on deck. They started repairs before the insurance company paid a dime, actually before they even sent out their own experts. When the insurance company's engineers finally showed up, they simply signed off on everything without a fight. The repairs were already moving along quickly. They didn't try to control the process now that construction was underway and there were knowledgeable experts already on-site. Suzanne had documented all the damage with photographs and kept detailed reports of the repair process. With our help, she was able to work with the insurance company adjusters to get the claim paid in full.

Of course, the insurance company can still dispute the claim or object to how repairs have been done. But they are much less likely to do so when repairs are underway and the policyholders have their own on-site experts. Even if they dispute the claim, you are better off fighting that battle while the repairs are already underway and your business isn't losing money, customers, and resources.

HOW TO PROTECT YOURSELF

In a better world, policyholders would be able to depend on their insurance company to pay claims accurately, fully, and promptly. But we don't live in a better world. In this world, you cannot assume that the insurance company will pay your claim fairly or timely. You cannot assume that their experts and estimators are on your side or that they will give an accurate and unbiased estimate.

However, there are things that businesses can do to protect themselves.

First, establish lines of credit ahead of time, *before* a potential loss, so that you can finance repairs on your own. Getting credit after a major disaster, such as a hurricane or earthquake, can be difficult. Everyone wants credit when a major disaster strikes, which can create liquidity issues for the banks, assuming they are even open in the days and weeks following a disaster. Your banker will want to see your insurance policy, but quick money cannot be counted on from the insurers issuing the policy.

Second, hire your own experts. The insurance company's experts are working for the insurance company, not you. They have most likely been selected because they are willing to represent the insurance company's interests. The insurance company may discourage you from hiring your own experts, as they don't want to deal with knowledgeable experts who are actually looking out for the policyholder, but that is actually why you should hire your own people and always have a second opinion.

Third, when a loss occurs, start mitigation repairs immediately if you can. Don't lose sales, clients, staff, or the whole business waiting on the insurance company to start doing its work. Just be sure to document everything, both the damage and the repairs, and have your contractors do the same.

Fourth, be proactive and assertive. Don't settle for less than you are owed. Don't let the insurance company bully concessions out of you. If you have taken the first three steps to start the repair process on your own, you have taken away the insurance company's leverage. This fact alone makes them less likely to delay payment or repairs. The insurance company is more likely to play the whole thing straight when you clearly have it together enough to get started on your own.

Fifth, ask for partial payments of agreed estimates of loss as they come due or are determined. Access to credit after a major loss can be a godsend, but you want to start repaying your creditors as soon as possible. Do not let the insurance company dangle partial estimates in front of you in order to gain concessions. You are owed the money. The insurance company should morally start making that undisputed money available as soon as possible. They don't need to finish the estimate to start paying what they already know they owe.

Finally, do your best to find a reputable insurance company that will treat you right. You cannot always depend on the insurance company, but you can still choose one that is reputable and known for taking care of commercial clients. While the bad faith practices described in this chapter are common to me because I get referred problem claims, there are good commercial insurance companies with solid reputations that pay claims without delays. They will likely charge more in premiums, but that's because you get what you pay for. Buy cheap insurance, and you may find out later that you are *not* getting what you *thought* you were buying. "Cheaper" insurance gets expensive when claims aren't paid promptly in full following a loss.

> "Cheaper" insurance gets expensive when claims aren't paid promptly in full following a loss.

Look for insurance companies that employ in-house engineering teams with risk management and loss avoidance as part of their culture. Ask for them to visit the property to set up a plan to prevent losses and a plan to get the business up and running again quickly in the event a loss happens. Great insurance companies foster this kind of culture and will be happy to do such things for their commercial clients. Purchasing insurance from the right insurer may just save you a huge headache and the pain of being out of business for months or longer—and if not, you should already be prepared to look out for yourself anyway.

CHAPTER 8

THE GOVERNMENT IS NOT IN THE BUSINESS OF COLLECTING INSURANCE BENEFITS

THE 2004 HURRICANE SEASON was particularly bad for Florida and much of the Gulf Coast region. There were sixteen tropical cyclones in the Atlantic that year, and half of them either landed in or brushed the United States. The four biggest hurricanes—Charley, Frances, Ivan, and Jeanne—all hit Florida. The following year, while many areas of Florida were still under repair, more tropical storms and hurricanes struck. In 2005, Hurricanes Rita and Katrina both glanced the southern part of Florida on their way to the Gulf. Then Hurricane Wilma came from the other direction, picking up steam in the Gulf before striking the state as a full-fledged hurricane. At the time, Wilma was the second-most-costly storm to ever hit Florida.

These storms resulted in widespread damage. Estimates place the 2004 losses around $42 billion. In 2005, losses exceeded $100 billion.

Many of these losses were supposed to be covered by insurance, but some policyholders found that their claims weren't getting paid quickly and often not in full.

This made a bad situation worse. Many homeowners were unable to return home because they couldn't get repairs paid or underway. Others with nowhere to go returned to water-damaged homes at their own peril. Many businesses with major damage couldn't reopen after the storm. Rental properties sat vacant for weeks that turned into months. When the insurance company won't pay a claim quickly, and commercial properties stay out of commission, losses start compounding rapidly.

Policyholders were understandably up in arms. In addition to filing lawsuits, many also filed complaints with regulatory bodies. Every state has its own department of insurance that takes consumer complaints. Some policyholders also called their government representatives to complain. This is a normal course of action when an insurance company isn't holding up its end of the bargain. Unfortunately, filing complaints with regulators and policymakers doesn't usually get claims paid. Government agencies aren't in the business of getting your claim paid. They're in the business of running the business.

Time and time again departments of insurance have proved largely ineffective at effectively regulating the insurance industry when it comes to wrongful claims conducted by insurers. Widespread bad faith practices aren't always enough to trigger a thorough investigation. And investigations aren't always timely enough to enact actual change when it is most needed. Following the hurricanes of 2004 and 2005, many policyholders with Allstate property insurance policies found this out the hard way.

ALLSTATE'S CORE CLAIMS REDESIGN PROCESS

Following the hurricanes in Florida, so many policyholders complained about Allstate not fully and promptly paying claims that the Office of Insurance Regulation, Florida's department of insurance, launched an inquiry into the company's claims practices. They "discovered" a pattern of delayed and undisputed claims. I put discovered in scare quotes because this is something that consumer advocates fighting on behalf of policyholders have known for a long time. I was intimately familiar with the culture of Allstate's claims departments. Our firm had pursued many cases against Allstate for bad faith practices regarding claims processing.

The ongoing problems with Allstate's claims department did not start in 2004. They can be traced back a decade before. Allstate was founded by Sears, Roebuck and Company in 1931 to sell automobile insurance by direct mail through the Sears catalog. Sears named the new subsidiary after its popular "Allstate" tire. By the time Allstate was spun off in 1993, it had grown into one of the nation's largest insurance providers. Allstate went through a major restructuring process following the spin-off. They brought in McKinsey & Company, a well-known corporate consultancy, to help the company redesign many of its processes and policies to increase profits.

McKinsey is famous for helping insurance companies restructure with a focus on bottom-line profit. McKinsey helped Allstate develop what became known as the Claims Core Process Redesign, a program designed to slash costs and payments in the claims department. McKinsey helped Allstate streamline and automate its entire claims process. They used data analytics to make claims decisions by algorithm. Adjusters could now plug the details of a claim into a computer system and get back a standardized course of action.

This automation process had at least two major problems. First, the algorithm wasn't always able to consider the nuances of and context surrounding a case. Second, the algorithm was tuned to lower costs. Rather than designing the system to pay claims accurately, it was designed to save Allstate money. There's nothing wrong with using data-driven analytics to save money, but there *is* something wrong with creating a system that intentionally avoids paying claims fully and fairly, which is exactly what Allstate was doing. They were looking for ways to save at the policyholders' expense.

The new system not only made recommendations about how much to pay but also whether to pay at all. Allstate used internal data to identify which cases should be settled quickly and which were better fought in court. Historically, most claims were settled without litigation. Allstate decided to see what would happen if they fought more cases in court. In one particularly egregious experiment, Allstate's West Palm Beach office declined to settle a *single* automobile insurance claim for three months. They took every last case to court just to see how this would affect the claims.

Allstate found that many people would rather abandon their cases than go to trial. Many people don't like speaking in public, especially before a court of law, and with many smaller claims, the cost of legal fees exceeds the disputed amount. In many cases, going to court isn't worth the effort or risk. You might have to pay court costs and still lose. Many people did. Having a legitimate case is no guarantee you will win the dispute. Many people lost due to having a subpar trial lawyer. Not everyone has access to a top-notch trial lawyer. Justice shouldn't depend on what kind of lawyer you can afford, but in practice it often does.

These practices were designed to get Allstate policyholders to abandon cases. The whole point was to save Allstate money at the policyholders' expense. And by that measure, the redesign was a resounding success. Costs came down. The claims department was paying less in benefits. Allstate was spending less on legal fees.

Of course, saving money to boost profits should not be the sole guiding principle of the claims department. The focus should be on paying claims accurately, not as cheaply as possible. But as long as insurance companies can get away with making money by adhering to wrongful claims practices, some unscrupulous insurers will do so.

And they were getting away with it. Allstate had been employing these tactics in Florida for a decade before the government finally started investigating why so many of the company's policyholders were filing complaints with the department of insurance. There was little regulatory oversight for a long time.

Things seemed poised to change in 2006 when Charlie Crist won the governorship on a platform that championed consumer protections for policyholders. He appointed better regulators, pushed a pro-consumer agenda in the legislature, and worked with the insurance commissioner, then Kevin McCarty, to start investigating companies like Allstate. Ultimately Allstate's Claims Core Process Redesign program came under scrutiny, and the department of insurance requested company documents related to the program as it related to property insurance. The Florida senate held hearings and placed similar requests of its own.

These documents would have been quite damning if made public. Allstate claimed they simply didn't exist. I knew this was not true for two reasons.

First, no company as big as Allstate massively overhauls its operations without leaving a paper trail. The program was built on data analytics. There would be reports on that data, as well as company memos about the new practices. Employees would need training materials on the new policies. There is no way to restructure a company without leaving a footprint. Companies don't throw out all these records.

Second, I knew the documents existed because I had seen many of them with my own eyes. We'd obtained copies of these documents through the discovery process while representing our own clients against these very practices over the years. We had fought many cases against the company over the bad faith practices implemented during the redesign.

Allstate rolled out the Claims Core Process Redesign in the mid-1990s with many of its medical liability and automobile liability insurance policies. This helped them test out the practices while flying somewhat under the radar. These policies pay a benefit to a third party rather than the policyholder, which has allowed bad faith practices to go undetected by regulators and consumer watchdogs and advocates. Policyholders get liability insurance to protect against financial ruin. We have the legal—and some would say moral—obligation to pay for the damage we cause others, which is why people buy liability policies. However, since the benefit goes to a third party, and disputes are between them and the insurance company, policyholders are less likely to file a complaint on a liability policy than they are under their own property insurance.

However, the third party would sometimes sue Allstate, and we were involved with a number of third-party attorneys who asked us to do bad faith cases. We also began to work on more and more cases involving property insurance as Allstate began applying the redesign program to its other insurance products. We had so many of these cases that we hired an attorney, Jerry Marvin, to work on nothing but bad faith cases against Allstate. He spent years litigating and battling Allstate. In the process, we acquired many documents from Allstate that exposed the bad faith practices of their Claims Core Process Redesign program.

At the time I was serving as the chair of the Bad Faith Insurance Litigation Group, part of the Association of Trial Lawyers of America (now known as the American Association for Justice), a pro-consumer group of lawyers. We worked together to advocate for policyholders whose claims had been wrongfully denied by sharing information and ideas. Unfortunately we couldn't share many of the Allstate documents that we obtained because they were under seal by court order. Allstate would routinely refuse to provide these documents and deny their existence, just as they were now doing with the Florida legislature, and would only begrudgingly hand them over by court order. They would seek a protective order that prevented us from sharing them with third parties. Allstate didn't want the documents made public and used in any of the other hundreds of open cases against them.

As the head of the Bad Faith Insurance Litigation Group, that was exactly what I wanted—to share these materials with other lawyers and policymakers working for and representing consumers, often Allstate's own customers. But to do so we would need documents that weren't sealed under protective orders. We needed to find documents that were in the public domain so that we could distribute them.

I had Jerry Marvin monitor newspapers and magazines, as well as court records and briefs, for any mention of lawsuits involving Allstate and the Claims Core Process Redesign. Every morning, first thing, he would scour the newsprint and pore over court papers looking for something we could share. One day, circa 1998, he hit pay dirt. A judge in Seattle had made Allstate turn over documents on the Claims Core Process Redesign as part of a discovery order. For whatever reason, there was no confidentiality clause. The materials were public record.

Another one of our attorneys, Charlie Hounchell, flew to Seattle and made copies of everything he could. This wasn't just written materials. There were also videos and tapes. There was a whole cache of useful materials that exposed the bad faith practices that McKinsey had helped Allstate develop. In fact, they even documented that McKinsey had advised Allstate to ignore consumer protections that the practices would run afoul of because the financial benefits and profits would outweigh the penalties and risk. We now had our evidence.

We were able to share these materials with other attorneys working on bad faith cases against Allstate. A decade later, our firm and the state legislators were also able to share them with Florida regulators investigating Allstate following the hurricanes. While these materials mostly dealt with medical and automobile liability policies, some of the documents indicated Allstate's intent to implement the same practices with their commercial and residential property insurance policies.

This was why I was certain that Allstate was hiding information from the Florida government. We were able to feed regulators and legislators much of this material, as well as our various court orders and public settlements from over the years, to help them build their case against Allstate. But they still needed the Claims Core Process Redesign documents that related directly to property insurance. I assured lawmakers and regulators that they existed but could not turn them over because they were under seal. When Allstate claimed otherwise, the state legislature and Office of Insurance Regulation knew better.

Florida policymakers and legislators insisted that Allstate hand over relevant documents on the claims process for their property insurance policies. They resisted, as usual, but a judge ordered the company to comply. Lawmakers sought a contempt order that would bar Allstate from operating in Florida entirely if the documents weren't produced by a specific date. Allstate had to follow state laws and regulations, as well as court orders, if they wanted to continue operating in Florida as an admitted carrier. Allstate tried to appeal the order but lost.

When the appeal was denied, Allstate finally gave up. The company made the material—some thirty thousand documents in all—publicly available online. The history and workings of the Claims Core Process Redesign and all its bad faith practices were now on display for all to see.

WINNING THE BATTLE WHILE LOSING THE WAR

This should have been a great victory for consumers. The documents were made public. The truth was revealed. Allstate had been exposed. The proof was finally out there for all to see. Regulators and lawmakers could now force the company to make changes to its operations. They could reform the entire industry.

But they didn't. The government did very little with the information they had uncovered. Policymakers had shown that they *could* regulate the industry and hold companies engaging in bad faith practices accountable, but they didn't actually follow through with doing so. They failed to hold Allstate fully accountable even though they had everything they needed to do so. The government should have conducted a detailed market study into Allstate's claims practices and performed a thorough inquiry. They should have been asking hard questions about individual cases. They should have scrutinized disputed claims and asked Allstate why they had denied them. They should have reviewed questionable practices and policies and insisted upon a change of culture. But none of that really happened after the initial hearings and the acquisition of the documents. Maybe they simply did not want to go through thirty thousand documents.

Florida lawmakers passed a few pro-consumer laws that would protect consumers from certain bad faith practices. Laws and regulations helping policyholders collect claims fully were enacted. Insurance companies operating in Florida are now required to pay claims more quickly so that they cannot hold the benefit hostage to extract concessions from policyholders. Repairs have to be made in a way that blends in with the rest of the structure. Other small consumer protections also passed.

However, these changes were made in a piecemeal fashion. Regulators didn't fundamentally reform the industry. Insurance companies still operate in mostly the same way they always have. They still operate under the same basic principle that maximizing profits comes first. And while there are slightly fewer bad practices that insurance companies can get away with, they still make it a point to get away with whatever they can. For the most part, it is still business as usual.

I once believed that exposing wrongdoing would lead to reform. The failure of regulators to hold Allstate accountable or reform the claims side of the insurance industry, even though they had all the proof in the world that consumers were being hurt in a routine and systematic manner, cured me of that naivety. Exposing wrongdoing alone isn't enough to protect consumers or ensure reform.

HOW TO PROTECT YOURSELF

When policyholders are treated unfairly by insurance companies, their natural inclination is to report the incident. Each state has its own department of insurance that is supposed to regulate the insurance industry and look out for consumers and their interests. These offices have a department that hears consumer complaints.

But is anyone really listening? Is anyone acting upon tips or addressing complaints? Are there mechanisms in place for regulators to actually address consumers' concerns? Is there the political will to act?

From my experience, the answers vary widely from state to state and depending on the claims. Many states do fantastic work on health insurance claims complaints but fail spectacularly when confronted about a commercial property claim. Some place emphasis on getting disaster claims paid quickly and in full but lack the resources to handle the many run-of-the mill claims that arise every day.

Is anyone acting upon tips or addressing complaints? Are there mechanisms in place for regulators to actually address consumers' concerns? Is there the political will to act?

Ultimately you cannot depend on government agencies to get your claim paid. Bureaucrats are in the business of running bureaucracies, not chasing down your insurance benefits. In the best-case scenario, they will duly note your complaint and look for patterns of consumer abuse, but many won't actually help you get your claim paid. The insurance commissioner is not there to collect on your claim. Bureaucrats aren't consumer advocates. Getting your claim paid, no matter how legitimate, is not in their job description as far as they are concerned.

Regulators may not even be sympathetic with consumers. In most states, insurance commissioners are appointed. The position is often filled by insurance industry insiders who are more likely to be on the side of the insurance companies than the consumer. But even the best insurance commissioners cannot track down every claim. That's not their job. They don't have the resources, and that's not what they are there for. To get your claim paid, you might have to be proactive and take matters into your own hands.

First, you *should* file complaints with your state's department of insurance. These agencies are supposed to regulate the industry. They can't protect consumers from bad faith practices unless they are aware of them. Insurance companies work hard to keep these practices secret. They will do everything in their power to cover their tracks and withhold evidence. Regulators aren't always aware of the bad faith practices that occur. Filing a complaint at least gives regulators the *chance* to address the issue. There's no downside to filing a complaint, and there might, just maybe, be an upshot. There are some good people working in government who may try to help.

Second, reach out to consumer advocates and attorneys working to protect consumers. They can act as a megaphone that can get your complaint heard. I have been advocating for policyholders for more than thirty years now. My blog at www.propertyinsurancecoveragelaw.com is read by both regulators and insurance industry insiders. We use the platform to expose bad faith practices. This helps keep policymakers and regulators abreast of what is happening in the industry and also encourages insurance companies to clean up their act.

Talking to a consumer advocate can also help you understand your rights, what you are entitled to, and whether you have a case worth pursuing. You should always talk to a lawyer or consumer advocate if the insurance company isn't treating you fairly, especially if your claim isn't getting paid, before signing anything. Insurance companies will often make lowball offers and have policyholders sign a release that precludes them from seeking further compensation when they find out that the repairs are going to cost more than they thought. Don't sign any release until you have talked to experts who are on the side of consumers.

Insurance policies are a contract between you and the insurer. If you feel like the insurance company isn't living up to their end of the bargain, get a second opinion from an expert.

CHAPTER 9

WHY CAN'T WE ALL GET ALONG?

CONDOMINIUMS, HOTELS, AND APARTMENTS ARE DIFFERENT INSURING BREEDS OF CAT

IN THE 1990s Monaco Gardens Condominiums discovered a massive sinkhole forming beneath the property. The sinkhole threatened two buildings if the ground continued to collapse underneath them. A repair was needed right away. The condominium association filed a claim with Allstate only to have it denied. The condominium association then hired me to represent them in the matter. We had our own engineers examine the property and confirm the presence of the sinkhole. Allstate finally conceded that the sinkhole existed, but we couldn't come to a consensus on how to have it fixed.

Allstate wanted to fix the sinkhole by pumping the ground full of grout at high pressure. The grout would raise the land back up and the pressure would compact the soil to provide a more stable surface. This was the cheapest way of addressing the issue, but not necessarily a permanent solution. While grout will fill in sunken cavities and stabilize the soil for a time, the dried grout can shift over years and decades as the earth around it continues to erode. Given the sinkhole's proximity to the buildings, our engineers recommended putting in steel piles to anchor the building foundations to the bedrock beneath before pumping in grout. Running piles through the grout keeps it from shifting over time. This would create a more permanent solution, but it would also cost more. Allstate didn't want to pay for steel piles, only the grout.

We sent a complaint to the insurance commissioner's office to get Allstate to pay for the piles. However, Allstate preempted the complaint by exercising their right to perform the repair. Virtually all property insurance policies give the insurer the option of actually doing the repairs. This allows the insurance company more control over how repairs are done. Insurers rarely invoke this clause because they then become guarantors of the construction, but it also allows them to take control of the repair costs

There was little we could do to stop Allstate from making the repairs themselves. Electing to make the repair was within their legal rights under the policy. They sent out a construction crew and started pumping grout. Things did not go so well for Allstate. Low-mobility grout flows slowly, so the process would take several days. On the third day, I got a panicked call from Monaco Garden's property manager. The grout was migrating through cracks and openings in the loose soil and traveling to a field of public water wells all the way on the other side of the highway. Grout was literally coming up out of the wells.

The next day, I got a call from Richard Wilson, an attorney representing Allstate. He said I had probably heard that the compaction grout project wasn't going as planned. Indeed I had. Wilson said that Allstate was willing to pay the claim up to the policy limit. In fact, Allstate's policy required it to pay 150 percent beyond the policy limit. They didn't want to finish the repairs.

I said thanks, but no thanks. They had exercised their option to repair the property and fix the sinkhole rather than pay the claim. That decision was not revocable on a whim. Allstate was now required to finish the repairs, no matter the cost. Allstate had dug themselves into a hole (pun intended) by starting the grout. If the sinkhole stretched all the way to China, that was now their problem. They had to finish the job.

Of course, we didn't actually want them to finish the job. The grout-only method was not the right fix. But this gave us leverage, and we were able to get a generous settlement that would more than pay for the repairs and then some to take care of my attorney's fees.

FROM SETTLEMENT TO LAWSUIT

This was a happy ending for the Monaco Gardens condominium association and its members, right?

Not so fast. Long after the settlement with the insurer, I learned that fights broke out within the association. Members of the condo association started fighting over the settlement money, how it should be spent, and to whom it should go. Everyone wanted a piece of the pie. Even people in units and buildings wholly unaffected by the sinkhole started coming out of the woodwork to argue for a slice of the settlement.

There was no system in place to prevent or even handle this conflict. Once the fighting began, no one trusted the other members. They didn't trust the association. They started filing lawsuits against each other. They sued the association. I was called in to give a public deposition. The whole thing was sad to watch. These people had just won a very fair and generous settlement and were now wasting their own money on suing each other. Court costs and legal fees ate away at the settlement money they had obtained.

Human nature being what it is, this was an unfortunate situation but wholly predictable. People are self-interested. Just because people are on the same side of the dispute before the money comes in doesn't mean they will be afterward. This is an inherent difficulty with insurance claims that involve multiple parties. Policies covering condominiums and other multiunit housing are different from single-family detached homes. People who own their own units also share a common roof, common walls, common utility systems, common infrastructure behind the walls, and common areas. Disputes over parts of the claim may affect individual members differently.

> **Making decisions about how to handle claims and dividing up the benefit in advance is critical. People can be quite unreasonable once real money is on the table.**

Anyone managing or overseeing the affairs of a condominium association or its board needs to understand that members will sometimes be at odds and plan accordingly when making choices about insurance and repairs. This is especially true for large, expensive condominium buildings, where claims can easily stretch into the tens of millions of dollars, and there might be hundreds of parties involved with the claim. This creates the potential for a lot of high-stakes conflict. With this many people under the same roof, you can almost guarantee that someone will fight about anything and everything, up to and including the roof itself.

While you cannot prevent all conflict, you can create an environment that makes conflicts easier to manage. Prepare for problems before they happen. Making decisions about how to handle claims and dividing up the benefit in advance is critical. People can be quite unreasonable once real money is on the table. Money clouds reasonable people's judgment. My only job was to obtain the insurance settlement money. But I wish I had worked more with their association counsel to prepare him for the possibility of a large sum of money being obtained.

Condominium associations should have a plan in place—and in writing—for how claims and insurance lawsuits will be handled. Know how claims will be pursued and settlements divided and dispersed. Have a trustee already in place as well as an agreed-upon manner for handling disputes so that expensive lawsuits may be avoided. You don't want members turning on each other nor some gold diggers seeing a pot of treasure from a large settlement.

When a loss does happen, the association should do its best to stick to the plan while also managing unseen eventualities as they occur. Unexpected situations can always arise, but stick to the script as much as possible. Be as transparent as possible about the whole insurance claim process so that members trust the process and the board of directors. Keep knowledgeable and specialized condominium retainers to help prevent these disputes from escalating. Engineers and architects should work to oversee the repair process in a way that accounts for the interests and respects the rights of individual members as well as the association as a whole.

DON'T FALL VICTIM TO UNINFORMED GROUPTHINK

Infighting isn't the only peril that condo associations face when trying to get an insurance claim paid. Sometimes the association can come to a consensus on the wrong course of action. With many parties to the suit all pushing for the same thing, even good legal counsel and experts may be hard pressed to hold back the tide of popular opinion.

This is what almost happened to the condominium association of Three Palms Pointe, a large waterfront multibuilding condominium complex in St. Petersburg, Florida. Continual exposure to moisture, along with salt from the seawater, caused the balconies and the steel structure behind the fascia to start rusting. The hidden decay actually threatened the structural integrity of the buildings.

The property was insured by State Farm, which sent out engineers to look at the building. They confirmed the rust damage and agreed that it was covered under the policy. However, State Farm kept disputing the figures put forth by the association's experts based on other experts it had hired. The association was being represented by Dick Tutwiler, a top-notch public adjuster in Florida, who had hired a structural engineer who originally estimated the cost of repairs at approximately $3.6 million.

After disputes about the costs, I was also retained as their legal counsel. The board asked me to see if State Farm would settle for approximately $2 million so that construction could start quickly. This seemed like the association selling itself short, but they wanted to move along. Ultimately my feelings were moot. State Farm refused even the $2 million figure.

Throughout this process, we were still inspecting the property. I went back to the building with Dick Tutwiler and the engineer to get a more thorough assessment. I also brought another forensic engineer. He cut a hole in the fascia and reached inside. We all watched as he pulled out a handful of rust. The problem was much worse than we had first thought. After performing a survey of parts of the building and extrapolating out, our engineers estimated the cost of repairs at $5.5 million.

I took this new estimate back to State Farm along with documentation of the hidden damage in the walls for them to review. I explained that this was only a theoretical amount and that the damage could be even worse, but since the condominium association wanted to do the repairs quickly, this is what we were asking for now. At this point, State Farm had the gall to ask if we would accept the $3.6 million from the first estimate. Of course we said no. That offer was off the table. We now knew the damages were much higher.

> Every time we discovered more damage, they would try to get us to accept an estimate they had previously declined.

Three Palms Pointe hired contractors to start the repairs while the dispute worked its way through arbitration. The more engineers and construction crews went through the building, the more rust damage they encountered. The price tag just kept climbing. The next estimate was $8.5 million. At this point, State Farm asked if we would be willing to take the $5.5 million! Every time we discovered more damage, they would try to get us to accept an estimate they had previously declined.

The fact that the units were occupied added to the cost of repair. The majority of occupants were elderly. Many were in wheelchairs and had mobility issues. Working around them was slow and tedious for the contractors, which added significantly to the cost. We came up with a plan to rotate residents out of their units and into hotel rooms while the contractors worked on those units. Doing the repairs this way would actually save the insurance company $2 million in labor costs. However, the work was still not going to be cheap. By this time, we had a thorough estimate of the whole building. Even with the savings, we now put the total cost at $12.1 million.

The insurance company rejected this final figure too. We then went into an arbitration trial, where the association was awarded $11.3 million. However, State Farm refused to pay for the cost of relocating the residents and their property out of the building during the repair process, which came to $1.26 million, even though it ultimately saved them even more off the total figure. They argued that relocation costs were not covered under the policy.

We now had to go back to court to argue that while State Farm wasn't directly required to pay relocation costs under the policy, they were required to cover the cost of mitigation efforts. The total bill would have been much higher if we hadn't relocated the residents. The trial judge agreed with this argument and also ruled that State Farm could only challenge the entire arbitration award, not just the pieces they didn't like, precisely to avoid this problem. State Farm appealed the decision up to the Eleventh Circuit Court of Appeals but lost the appeal with written opinions about why it was wrong!

The condominium association ultimately collected its claim, plus interest and attorney's fees, but doing so took two and a half years of wrangling. I remember many of the tenants telling me at the outset that they weren't sure they would live two more years, which is why they wanted to settle quickly. But settling quickly would have meant taking less than $2 million instead of over $11 million. The condominium association would then have been on the hook for the other $9 million in yet-to-be-discovered damages if they had signed a release rather than do a complete analysis and fight.

There are two lessons here. First, don't accept a settlement without fully investigating the damage. Do your due diligence before agreeing to a full settlement. The insurance company should be willing to do a partial estimate and start paying for known losses while the full estimate is completed. But don't ever sign a release until you know the full extent of the damage to the best of your ability.

Second, do not allow an association or group to succumb to group pressure to accept an early lowball offer. Many insurance companies are conveniently slow to find the total estimate. Mind the long game and be sure that *everything* is being fixed correctly in a first-rate manner.

When so many people are involved in a claim, some of them are likely to want to resolve the issue and collect benefits as quickly as possible. Members of a group have different motivations. Having so many parties involved in the claim can lead to groupthink or pressure from parties that aren't immediately affected. There is a lot that can go wrong behind the walls of large multiunit buildings. These problems can create a common problem for the entire building, not just one unit, which means that the claims-and-repair process for the whole building needs to be handled holistically.

Finally, make sure that you have experts who can help you determine the entire loss accurately. This is critical for large claims. You should hire your own engineers and public adjusters as well as attorneys with experience in these kinds of claims to perform an estimate and oversee the claims process. Don't trust the insurance company experts and adjusters. They work for the insurance company's interests, not yours.

TENANTS AND WORKERS HAVE RIGHTS TOO

Condominiums aren't the only places where people share space. Hotels, apartments, and even office buildings all have people sharing space under one roof. While tenants and renters are generally not parties to the insurance policy covering the building, they do have rights that must be considered after a loss. When offering a lease, you are promising to provide a safe space to the lessee. You cannot have people living or working in unsafe conditions. Failing to keep them abreast of and safe from hidden dangers may subject the owner, landlord, or property manager to civil or criminal penalties.

When a building suffers damage, the lessor needs to consider the lessee's needs. Water damage isn't just a problem for the building. It is a problem for the people who live there. Living around mold can cause permanent health problems. You need to get people out of dangerous environments. This is something that may be covered under your policy or may be considered as part of mitigation, as it was in the case of Three Palms Pointe.

When you are doing repairs, you have to consider the occupants. Will the repairs disturb asbestos? Will they create dangerous noise levels? Will they compromise the structure of the building? Do the utilities need to be shut off during the construction? Are repairmen trusted enough to enter others' units or workspaces? Any of these things can require moving people out or changing how the work is done, which will affect the cost of repair and value of the claim.

These considerations aren't limited to apartment buildings. Hotel proprietors are faced with similar considerations about guests. Some hotels rent by the week or month, making the guests short-term tenants, and even hotels that only rent by the night have to decide whether guests can stay safely. Keeping these guests safe is a legal and moral obligation. The same is true for workers, who must be provided with a safe working environment per OSHA guidelines. Violating these guidelines or tenants' rights can result in lawsuits or even criminal penalties. Don't ignore the rules just to keep the business running.

The point here is that damaged large multiunit properties with many people living or working under the same roof make for complicated losses. They deserve the consideration and oversight of experienced experts. The larger the property, the more involved the repairs can be. The more parties involved, the more complicated the claim. This makes claims regarding large losses at condominiums, hotels, apartments, office buildings, and other multiunit buildings inherently more complex than those dealing with single-family detached homes. These large losses are a whole other beast under the eyes of the law and have to be treated differently during the adjustment phase.

HOW TO PROTECT YOURSELF

Condominium associations, boards, property managers, hotel proprietors, and anyone else overseeing the insuring of a multiunit building need to understand that these policies are different. They need to protect themselves against the problems that can arise when you have so many parties affected by a loss and claim.

First and foremost, plan ahead so that you know what to do when a loss occurs. Understand your policy and how losses and repairs will affect unit owners, tenants, employees, and guests. Know how repairs will be handled so that safety is first. Understand who will oversee and disperse money, as well as how it will be dispersed. Know who will work with contractors and oversee their work so it is done safely, properly, and on time.

Second, be as transparent as possible with everyone involved and keep lines of communication open. Association members should not be kept in the dark about the claim. Residents, tenants, and guests should be informed of all possible dangers. Keep all parties abreast of how claims, litigation, arbitration, and repairs are progressing, as appropriate. People get distrustful when they feel shut out of the process. Simple transparency can help keep people from complaining, making rumors, or suing each other.

Third, make sure you have experts on hand who can ensure that you are following the proper regulations and getting everything that the whole group deserves. Large properties usually have general counsel who can help guide owners or associations through many of these practical and general issues, but those running or owning smaller properties are not exempt from all the rules.

Fourth, hire your own experts as well. This is especially true for large multiunit properties suffering a large loss. You cannot always trust the insurance company's experts, adjusters, or engineers. They aren't there to make sure that the work gets done properly. They are there to make sure it gets done as economically as possible. They have an incentive to turn a blind eye to problems that might arise down the road. Getting the insurance company to pay years later will be much more difficult, if not impossible. You want to make sure that repairs are done right the first time. Failing to do repairs properly can result in residents, whether they are tenants, unit owners, workers, or guests of owners, filing lawsuits against you in the future.

CHAPTER 10

CAN YOU TRUST YOUR INSURANCE AGENT?

IN A PREVIOUS CHAPTER, I mentioned joining Suzanne Harris of the Edgewater Beach Owners' Association at speaking engagements focused on property insurance for condominium owners and associations. A common topic at these talks is the need to hire a good insurance agent. *Good* is the operative word here. A good agent can help policyholders understand their own unique insurance needs so that no gaps in insurance go uncovered.

Educated and practical advice is what a good agent can offer you. A bad agent? Don't count on anything.

This very topic came up when I joined Suzanne on stage in Orlando at a conference hosted by the Community Associations Institute. We talked about the importance of finding an insurance agent you can trust. Suzanne urged anyone buying property insurance for condominiums to find an agent who works hard to understand your specific needs and liabilities. The unsung value of a good agent is covering any and all risks of loss, even those you don't know you have. Going with a less-than-stellar agent can result in coverage gaps you weren't expecting.

At one point, Suzanne locked eyes with someone in the crowd. "We actually have an audience member here tonight that knows all about this, isn't that right?"

The man in the crowd gave a knowing smile.

I was with Suzanne at the front of the room. "How do you know he knows that?"

"Because I sued him over it," she said. "He was our insurance agent."

Several years before, the man had helped her condominium association insure the Edgewater Beach condominium that Suzanne oversees. Unfortunately he'd neglected to insure the fences on the property. Fencing is rarely covered under a typical property insurance policy and usually has to be insured under a separate supplemental policy and by an endorsement. The agent hadn't offered such a policy, so when the fencing was destroyed, the insurance company refused to cover restoration. The association sued the agent and won. Before buying the policy, Suzanne gave him a copy of the association's bylaws, which clearly stated the fencing needed to be insured. The fences would have been insured were it not for his negligence.

The agent had no hard feelings, which is why he attended her talk. The incident had taught him the importance of attention to detail and ultimately made him a better agent. For her part, Suzanne also learned something. She now has her insurance agents read and sign a checklist of things to review, including the association's bylaws, to ensure that the agent doesn't miss anything. Also, in the event of a legal dispute, the signed checklist is proof that the association instructed the agent on what to cover.

This checklist is a great idea. These kinds of mistakes happen all the time. Even small mistakes can have big implications. Suzanne

Harris only had to contend with her fences not being covered—just imagine an oversight that prevented the actual building, which suffered significant damage, from being covered. For instance, having property listed under a wrong name on the policy can result in your claim not getting paid. This is common with small family businesses, which might not be titled in the owner's name, and agents don't always catch it.

These risks are not limited to business property only. I once represented a divorcée whose house burned down in a fire. Her agent failed to put the policy in her name after her ex-husband moved out. The house was not covered, although it was still titled in both of their names. Ironically, the insurance company agreed to cover personal items that her ex-husband had left behind, just not any of her possessions nor the house. I helped her sue the insurance company to no avail. She wasn't on the policy and wasn't entitled to benefits. The judge refused to reform the policy to reflect her interest. We ultimately sued their agent. He had known about the divorce and had even changed automobile policies. He should have helped her update the homeowner policies. We won that lawsuit, but the whole hassle could have been avoided if the agent had done his due diligence or if the couple had used a better agent who paid more attention to detail.

Ideally, you never want to sue your insurance agent. What you want is for them to make sure you have the best available coverage that meets all your insurance needs. You want them to dot all the i's and cross all the t's so that when it comes time to make a claim, it gets paid rather than resulting in your facing some technical loophole that could have been avoided.

NOT ALL AGENTS ARE THE SAME

The moral of these stories isn't that you can't trust your agent. The lesson here is to find an agent you can trust.

The moral of these stories isn't that you can't trust your agent. The lesson here is to find an agent you can trust. When people ask me if they should trust their insurance agent, I turn it around on them and ask: *Do* you trust your insurance agent?

While a good agent is a valuable asset, there are plenty of bad ones looking to make a quick buck and move on. They don't take the time to learn your needs. They may not know all the available options, and even if they do, they may have a vested interest in keeping them from you. Not all agents have access to the same insurance products. Unscrupulous agents might sell you a product that they can offer rather than recommend one better suited for you that they cannot.

There are generally three types of agents: captive agents, independent agents, and surplus lines brokers.

Captive agents only sell insurance products from a single insurance company. They cannot sell policies from competitors and won't recommend them. They can be very useful, since some great insurance companies, such as Amica, only sell policies through their captive agents. And while captive agents cannot speak to the competitors' products, they are usually very knowledgeable about the products they do sell.

Independent agents contract with multiple insurance companies. They may be able to offer a wider range of products because they work with more insurance companies. However, they still won't be able to sell policies from all insurance companies, only those they work with.

Surplus lines brokers typically sell niche policies or custom insurance packages for hard-to-place risks. They can be useful when you have unusual or complex insurance needs. They may be ideal for large businesses that need help devising customized insurance plans. They are also commonly used by very wealthy people with complex insurance needs. Your own agent will have to contact a surplus lines broker because they deal only with insurance agents and not the public. While there are drawbacks to buying surplus lines coverage, namely that the state won't guarantee the policy and pay your claim if the insurance company goes belly up, there is sometimes no other way to cover certain unusual or high-risk liabilities that captive and independent agents refuse to cover.

This is why using a good agent you can trust is so important. Find an agent that is knowledgeable, experienced, and willing to put in the time to understand your unique insurance needs. Being an insurance agent is a significant calling. Insurance companies constantly change their policies. Keeping up with the changes and available products is a huge undertaking. On top of that, insurance agents must understand the idiosyncratic needs of each policyholder. Great agents should also be willing to put the interests of the customer above their own or that of the insurance company and provide honest and accurate advice.

Some bad agents aren't just bad—they're con artists. Be wary of lone agents who operate one-man shops. There are definitely good agents who work alone. However, most fraud perpetrated by insurance agents is done by sole practitioners or smallish shops working alone. Vet these people extra carefully.

I once had a client on the New Jersey Shore who purchased workers' compensation insurance for his company through an insurance agent who worked alone. My client found the agent through a friend of a friend and failed to vet him properly. My client paid monthly premiums for five years before filing a claim over an injured worker. Then he discovered that the agent had never actually purchased the policy. He had been pocketing the monthly premiums. In an attempt to cover up the fraud, the so-called agent hired actors to play insurance adjusters and even an attorney.

This was a particularly bizarre case, but more mundane cases of fraud can occur. Be hypervigilant when selecting an agent, and make sure you are getting someone trustworthy and dedicated to the profession.

Good agents are those who earn your trust by being ethical, knowledgeable, and experienced. They look out for the policyholder. They pay attention to details. They understand the provisions and fine print of the policies they sell. For instance, many snowbirds are shocked to realize that their policies don't cover theft when they aren't actively living at a property. Many policies won't cover burglaries at your Manhattan apartment while you're down in Arizona for the winter, even if you're paying premiums on time. Many policies have loopholes that allow the insurer to get out of paying claims. Great agents know the circumstances of your lifestyle and find policies and insurers that will cover you while avoiding these loopholes.

All kinds of fine details and provisions are hidden in policies that can prevent a claim from getting paid. Everyone *should* read their policies, but generally people don't. Even when we do, the fine print and legalese might as well be Greek to most people. Instead, just about everybody relies on agents to help them understand policies and get the right coverage. They depend on agents to understand the policies they sell. Good agents do understand the policies they sell, but others don't even read the policies themselves.

Good agents also don't disappear after you sign the contract and pay your premium. The best agents will continue to be your advocate and help guide you with the claims process. They will serve as a liaison between you and the insurance company. When a claim is filed, they are there to help walk you through the process. Great agents are your front line when dealing with the insurance claims department. In today's insurance claims environment, policyholders need good advocates who understand what they are selling.

Above all, great agents work hard to learn *your* specific insurance needs. They will take time to ask questions about your property, your business, your health, your lifestyle, and whatever it is you are trying to insure. Good business insurance agents should know your business inside and out, as well as your industry, so that they can anticipate possible future losses and ensure you have the proper coverage. They understand that life and business are in constant flux, and they will revisit your policies on a periodic basis to make sure you still have the right coverage.

The nature of life is that we tend to accumulate more property as we age. The wealthier you are, the more you have to lose. The more property you own, the bigger your business, the more exposure you have. Everyone should get the insurance they need and can afford (and if you can't afford insurance, you can't afford the liability); but the more wealth you accumulate, the greater your liability and risk of loss. As you become more successful and affluent, it becomes exponentially more important to get the right insurance package. And for most people and businesses, finding the right insurance package starts with finding the right agent.

HOW NOT TO FIND AN AGENT

So how do you find a good agent? Let's start with how you shouldn't go about it.

First, do not shop on price alone. Agents with the lowest-cost products do not necessarily have the best products, much less the best products for *you*. Price is not an indication of value. Insurance companies can easily bring down premiums by simply covering less. Cheaper policies might include exclusions and provisions that result in less being paid in benefits.

A good agent helps you understand what will and won't be covered under different policies. They take the time to learn your needs and find policies that cover your risks. A bad agent will happily sell you cheap products to make a quick buck, pocket the commission, and move on to the next customer. You may even be tempted to brag about the price of this "cheap" insurance. But you get what you pay for. Cheap insurance is rarely, if ever, a good deal. Do not fall into the price trap.

Second, do not rely on referrals alone. Most people find agents by word of mouth. Not knowing anything about insurance products, some customers are happy for any referral, even if it comes from a friend's half cousin twice removed. Do not be tempted to select the guy who belongs to your golf club. We buy insurance to protect against the worst and hope for the best. Most of the time, the worst doesn't happen, and policyholders never file a claim. But it's only once you have a claim paid that you know for sure whether you have the coverage you *think* you do. Pick an agent that is a true professional with the qualifications to prove it—not somebody's friend or relative.

FINDING THE RIGHT AGENT FOR YOU

Now, there's nothing wrong with looking for the best deal. There's also nothing wrong with following up on recommendations from personal or business contacts. You just need to vet referrals like you would anyone else. Make sure that prospective agents are knowledgeable experts who can be trusted to take care of your insurance needs.

There are several things to look for when considering an agent.

First, check their credentials. You want an agent who has gone above and beyond to learn the trade. In most states, getting licensed as an agent is as simple as taking a short course, typically only six to eight weeks long, passing a test, and getting a surety bond. Look for something more. There are Certified Insurance Counselors (CICs), Chartered Property and Casualty Underwriters (CPCUs), agents with Associate in Risk Management (ARM) degrees, Accredited Advisors on Insurance (AAIs), and more. You will need to do some research to find out what credentials agents working your locale and area of insurance should have. Because these credentials might be numerous and confusing, consider consulting independent bodies that vet and certify agents, such as Trusted Choice, which operates across the nation. These organizations can help you find reputable agents with the right credentials.

Second, seek out agents who are involved in professional organizations. Large businesses should seek out agents in positions of leadership in the insurance agent profession. Find the major insurance associations in your state and see who is on the board of directors. These people will be leaders in the field and command the respect of their colleagues and peers. They are usually extremely knowledgeable. You may not need a leader in the field just to buy a homeowners insurance policy, but businesses or people who need extremely large policies should consider looking for the top agents in their area.

Third, look for agents who specialize in the type of insurance you need. Some agents specialize in business insurance, while others sell individual policies. Health insurance is different from life insurance, and business insurance is different from homeowners insurance. Most agencies have specialists in different fields. Find an agent who works in the type of insurance you need and who understands the area. For example, art collectors shouldn't just get any property insurance agent—they should find one with experience insuring collectibles and fine art.

Such considerations become critical for business insurance. Your agent should be experienced working with your industry. Law firms want agents who work with law practices on an exclusive basis. Financial firms want agents who know the financial industry. This specialization is critical to your agent's ability to cover risks you don't even know you have.

The vast majority of business owners know they need to cover their property in case of a loss. Most even know they should get coverage for business interruption in case a loss interrupts business operations. However, not everyone thinks about more obscure liabilities like the interruption of a dependent business. Can you operate after a supplier goes down in a disaster even though your business is untouched? If a beachfront restaurant goes unscathed in a hurricane but all the hotels in the area close their doors, the restaurant, dependent on customers from the hotels, will undergo a huge loss unless it is covered by insurance. Without dependent business coverage, the restaurant has a major uncovered risk—one the owner may never have considered. Specialized agents have been around the block often enough to anticipate these kinds of losses.

Fourth, get the right type of agent for you. Most people looking for individual property insurance can go to an independent agent at a small agency. However, very affluent people might want to seek out risk managers who can craft a customized insurance package to meet unusual and complex needs. They can help affluent people cover things like private jets or boats. Likewise, while small businesses can go to a smaller agency, large corporations should seek out large agencies and brokers that cater to their industry. The more complex your insurance needs, the more experienced and specialized your agent or team of agents should be.

THE BEST OFFENSE IS A GOOD DEFENSE

One of the best insurance agents I have ever known is Bill Wilson, who authored the book *When Words Collide*. In the book, Bill explains that the primary job of insurance agents and risk managers is to help people get good coverage that won't result in disputes. He also believes that when disputes do happen, good agents should help their clients navigate the claims process in a way that avoids litigation. In essence, he believes the value of a good agent keeps you from needing the services of a good attorney.

As an insurance attorney fighting against bad faith insurance practices, I couldn't agree with him more. You don't want to come see me. I spend my days helping policyholders with denied and underpaid claims get the benefits they are due. People and businesses only see me when something goes terribly wrong. Ideally, policyholders will get the coverage they need and have their claims paid quickly and fully without ever needing to involve an attorney. A good agent who gets you the right insurance from the right carrier, guides you through the claims process, and serves as your first and best advocate gives you the best shot at never needing a good lawyer.

CHAPTER 11

DEALING WITH THE NEW LOSS PROFESSIONALS: PUBLIC ADJUSTERS, LOSS CONSULTANTS, AND CONTRACTORS

I ONCE GOT A CALL from Dick Tutwiler, the public adjuster I mentioned in Chapter 9, about an optometrist whose office had burned to the ground. Dick was one of the first public insurance adjusters to start sending me referrals after I stopped representing insurance companies. He is also one of the best in his profession. Policyholders hire public adjusters to represent them during the claims process. The insurance company has its own adjusters who represent the company's interests. Public adjusters represent policyholders.

Dick wanted to run an idea by me about this client, whose entire medical practice was shut down after the fire. Dick's idea was for the optometrist to buy out another eye doctor's business and set up shop temporarily while repairs were done at the primary location. He wanted to double-check if the cost of the new location would be covered under his client's business interruption coverage. I told him it was unlikely the insurance company would pay for the whole business but that the policy should cover the cost of acquiring the temporary location.

"That's what I thought," Dick said.

His client purchased the temporary location and set up shop. The insurance company covered the cost of relocation and began working on restoring the original location. Meanwhile the optometrist retained most of his patients by moving them to the new temporary location. He also picked up many of the patients who had already been going to the prior doctor. The business was minimally interrupted, and any losses incurred were covered. There was also nothing stopping the doctor from keeping both locations once the repairs were completed. He actually came out ahead of where he would have been if the fire had never happened!

This wouldn't have been possible if the doctor hadn't sought out a top-notch public adjuster who knew these benefits were available under the insurance policy. Dick Tutwiler was able to use his knowledge of business interruption policies to turn a tragic situation into an opportunity. He called me for a second opinion, but the original idea was his. Without Dick, the doctor might have lost his patients and customers while waiting on repairs that could take the better part of a year. Instead, he actually grew his business.

This is an example of how a good public adjuster can advocate for policyholders from an informed position. The doctor had no idea what he was entitled to under his policy. He didn't know how to talk to the insurance company. He didn't know what was possible.

Dick did. Good public adjusters do this all the time.

THE VALUE OF A GOOD PUBLIC ADJUSTER

Hiring a public adjuster has several advantages.

First and foremost, they work for you and not the insurance company. Today most insurance company adjusters are under tremendous pressure to pay less in benefits. In a perfect world, all insurance adjusters assess claims accurately, cover losses in full, and ensure that policyholders get the entire benefit due. But we don't have a perfect world. In the real world, the insurance company claims managers often train adjusters to lower the company's obligations to you.

Second, public adjusters can help you through the claims process and make sure you meet your obligations on time. After suffering a loss, you are required to mitigate further losses and damage. You may have limited time to make a claim, file reports, challenge an assessment, or meet other obligations. Public adjusters guide you through this process and get paid to do much of it for you. Many people simply don't have the time to do these things themselves. Many business owners and homeowners don't have time to dig through the rubble after a structure burns down. Public adjusters return to the scene of the loss to prepare detailed estimates. They'll file paperwork to meet deadlines required by the policy.

Third, they have experience that customers do not. They understand the claims process and can guide policyholders through it. They are trained to look for and find hidden damage that may not be readily apparent. They know what policies typically cover and how to document a loss properly.

Fourth, they are better able to negotiate with the insurance company. Most policyholders simply aren't experienced and trained to negotiate the fairest deal with the insurance company. Insurance company adjusters are experts at getting claims settled as low as possible. You need an expert to make sure you get the full benefit due and that nothing is overlooked. Sometimes, as Dick Tutwiler was able to do for his optometrist client, they are able to get policyholders benefits they didn't know existed.

For these services, public adjusters charge either a flat amount or a percentage, often about 10 percent of the claim. That may sound like a lot, but public adjusters can often obtain you far more in benefits than the fees they charge.

Not getting a public adjuster has costs. Without a knowledgeable advocate, policyholders are more susceptible to being taken advantage of by the insurance company. Following a loss, policyholders want to get through the hassle of the claims process as quickly as possible. They often accept the insurance company's assessments and estimate at face value. Doing so can get the claim paid more quickly—but at what cost? Insurance company adjusters are often trained to lowball policyholders. They won't always inform policyholders of benefits they don't know they have.

Insurance company adjusters don't always alert the policyholder to the possibility of hidden damage that won't surface for weeks, months, or years. Water can hide behind walls and lead to mold problems that aren't immediately apparent. Toxins and particulates can hang in the air undetected. Drywall can hide structural damage that only becomes apparent as the building settles. Damage to insulation can lead to higher energy bills that might not be apparent until colder or warmer seasons.

Events that cause major property damage can lead to all kinds of secondary problems that policyholders cannot see right away. Sometimes the insurance company hides these problems. A coat of paint can hide quite a bit—for a little while. "Silver coat" may be applied to attics, literally spraying everything down with a coat of metallic paint, without first tearing out wet insulation. Sealing in the water can lead to mold and structural damage that the homeowner might not discover until trying to sell the house.

Experienced public adjusters know how to spot these problems. The insurance company's adjusters' job is to represent the insurance company, not you. Hiring a public adjuster allows you to keep tabs on the situation and what the insurance company is doing.

NOT ALL PUBLIC ADJUSTERS ARE GOOD ADJUSTERS

Of course, not all public adjusters are good at their jobs. There are even some very bad apples out there. In Florida, following Hurricane Andrew in 1992, we had lots of so-called public adjusters coming in from out of state. Some made false allegations on behalf of policyholders. There were stories about public adjusters sneaking into the loss site at night with crowbars and bashing things to make the damage look worse.

If true, such actions would have been criminal. They certainly weren't the norm, but they caught the attention of policymakers and legislators. The state considered banning public adjusters entirely. As a result, I was tapped by a community of insurance adjusters, whom I had worked closely with over the years, to help set up a statewide professional association of public insurance adjusters in Florida. Knowing that public adjusters are important policyholder advocates, I agreed to help alongside Douglas Grose, another attorney who is now with my law firm.

In 1993, we helped establish the Florida Association of Public Insurance Adjusters, now one of the largest public adjuster associations in the nation. I have worked with them for over twenty-five years now. We established a code of ethical conduct, an apprenticeship program, and more difficult and specialized statewide licensing require-ments. Thanks to these reforms, hiring a public adjuster in Florida has never been safer. Many other states now have enhanced licensing and educational requirements as well. I have nationally worked with these organizations from California to New Jersey. The best and most professional public adjusters call for high standards of conduct.

When hiring a public adjuster, perform due diligence and vet them properly. Make sure they are licensed. Check their credentials. Check to see if they participate in your state's professional organiza-tions for public adjusters. Generally, the best public adjusters are active in the field, are highly experienced, undertake continuing education, and work in leadership roles.

BEWARE OF SO-CALLED LOSS CONSULTANTS

Now that licensing requirements have improved, bad or unethical public adjusters are far less common than people merely pretending to be public adjusters. In most states, you cannot call yourself a public adjuster unless you are licensed. Some people have given themselves made-up titles like "loss consultants" or something similar. They claim to help policyholders with claims. However, without a license, these so-called loss consultants may be untrained and ineffective. In most states, only licensed public adjusters and practicing attorneys can legally negotiate or settle insurance claims for policyholders.

Unfortunately this doesn't stop unqualified "loss consultants" from setting up operations. Departments of insurance and state pros-ecutors routinely charge these people for practicing illegally, but there are always more in line to take their place. This is especially true following a major disaster. Buyer beware.

Make sure your public adjuster is actually a public adjuster. Anyone claiming to be a "loss consultant," "loss expert," or anything similar should raise a red flag in the mind of a policyholder. People filling this role should have the right credentials no matter what they call themselves. Some legitimate public adjusters will use these terms because they are easier for the public to understand. However, if they are real public adjusters, they will be licensed as such.

CONTRACTORS AS LOSS EXPERTS

Though rarely thought of as such, contractors are also loss experts. They are on the ground doing the actual work of repairing and restoring property after losses. They know as much, if not *more*, about certain aspects of the repair process for structures than actual adjusters. Hiring your own contractors, when possible, gives you control over who does the work. The insurance company's preferred contractors are often pressured to do cheap, subpar, and "just okay" repairs. The insurance company adjusters may still pressure your chosen contractor to cut corners, but this practice is still preferable to dealing with preferred contractors who depend on the insurance company for repeat business. Contractors so beholden to the insurance company are more easily pressured into doing subpar work.

> **Though rarely thought of as such, contractors are also loss experts.**

Reputable and quality-minded contractors can be valuable assets to policyholders. The average policyholder has no way of knowing when the construction work is done right. Construction and restoration are skilled trades. Using the wrong kind of roofing can result in problems in the future. Using the wrong nails on a particular shingle or failing to place the nails to spec can result in leaks or the roof being damaged in high winds or heavy rain. The details of construction matter—and the average policyholder simply does not have the expertise to recognize the fine details of quality construction. Good contractors do, which makes them experts in their specific domain. No one knows a quality roof repair better than a qualified and experienced roofer. When you hire your own contractors, so long as they are reputable, bonded, and willing to guarantee the work to manufacturers, you can better trust them to explain how to do the job right.

Even when you can pick your own contractors, the insurance company is still going to send out their adjusters to influence how repairs are made and the price to be paid. Good-quality contractors can push back and make sure that the work is done right. As compared to the average policyholder, experienced contractors are better equipped to insist that the job be done properly with quality materials according to the manufacturer's recommended methods.

To be clear: contractors *cannot* negotiate your claim with the insurance company. That's a job for you, a licensed public adjuster, or an attorney—no one else. However, contractors can serve as your eyes and ears on the ground. They can also advocate for you indirectly by doing work properly and in accordance with relevant laws. They can also let you know when work is not being done properly or according to regulations.

When looking for contractors, make sure they are licensed, bonded, credentialed, experienced, and reputable. They should have good references and years of experience. Unfortunately, finding good contractors after a major regional disaster can be difficult, as the best contractors are booked quickly.

You can also hire your own professionals to oversee the restoration process. Owners' representatives are found in planning, architecture, and engineering firms. You can hire them to be your on-site representative during the repair process and in many cases may even have the cost applied as a reasonable cost of construction. They are not there to manage the contractors. They are there to make sure that the contractors do their job right. Good contractors don't mind being observed. It's only contractors doing low-quality work

The larger the repair, the greater the need for your own representative on-site.

and cutting corners who don't want experts watching them. You can't always rely on government inspectors to ensure that construction is done properly and legally.

The larger the repair, the greater the need for your own representative on-site. The average policyholder doesn't know how construction is supposed to be done. You need a construction expert overseeing the repairs and making sure they are done to specifications and building codes. Commercial construction should always have representatives of the policyholder overseeing the work. Homeowners should also have representatives for major repairs. If your entire house is being gutted and rebuilt from top to bottom, you want the work done right by quality workers with your best interests in mind.

CHAPTER 12

THE ROLE OF POLICYHOLDERS IN THE CLAIMS PROCESS

AFTER SUFFERING A HOUSE FIRE, a Hispanic family living in the Miami area made the tragic mistake of signing a release form given to them by the insurance company. The form was written in English. They only spoke Spanish. They signed the form despite not being able to read a single word, believing that the insurance company adjuster just needed the paperwork filled out in order to get the insurance money to fix their home.

Unfortunately the insurance company didn't do right by them. It took complete advantage of the family. When hidden damages were discovered during the restoration process and additional funds were needed, the insurance company refused to pay. They cited the release form, which clearly stated that the policyholders were not entitled to any further compensation after signing the release. Of course the family hadn't actually been able to read that clause, but the insurance company didn't care.

The family called our law firm to explain the situation. The language barrier made it difficult to communicate. The policyholders' son tried to explain the situation in broken English. We sent Charlie Hounchell, an attorney in our office who was fluent in Spanish, to meet with them in person. After speaking with them, we were confident the release wouldn't hold up in court. Releases are only exchanged for something extra. The insurance company hadn't offered their customers anything in exchange for signing. They acted as if signing a release was a normal part of the property claims process, which it is not.

We filed a lawsuit and succeeded in getting the judge to throw out the release. The family recovered enough money to cover the additional repairs, as well as court costs, and their home was fully restored. However, despite the happy ending, they should never have signed the form in the first place. They had no idea what they were doing. Few policyholders do, which is why handling the claims process on your own is often a terrible idea.

This was an extreme case in which the insurance company tried to pull a fast one on particularly vulnerable policyholders who couldn't read the form. However, while the average policyholder *can* read English, they still *can't* understand legalese. They also don't know the relevant laws or the rights afforded them under statutes and requisitions. Most people can't make heads or tails of these kinds of documents or laws. They sign where they are told, especially when the insurance company is waving a check in front of them. All too often policyholders sign away their rights and benefits without realizing it.

NEVER TRY TO NAVIGATE THE CLAIMS PROCESS ALONE

Most policyholders should not try to navigate the claims process on their own. Do not be tempted to go it alone to save money. Doing so can mean not getting the full benefit to which you are entitled. In worst-case situations, you can be taken advantage of by the insurance company. You need experienced experts or professionals looking out for your interests.

The size and makeup of that team will depend on the policyholder, the type of policy, the size of the claim, whether there is a dispute with the insurance company, the amount of that dispute, and other factors. The bigger the claim and the larger the dispute—the more you need professionals on your team. Even with smaller claims on individual policies, the policyholder should pick up the phone to ask the insurance agent or broker for guidance. Your agent is your primary advocate before and immediately after a claim.

Larger and more complex claims require larger teams of experts from the start. This is especially true for commercial policyholders. Businesses may also include risk managers, accountants, in-house counsel, the chief financial officer (CFO), and other executives on the team. Large losses can affect any and all parts of a business, and there are legal and financial ramifications to decisions made around insurance coverage and claims.

No matter the size of your claim, the equation changes once a claim is denied, disputed, significantly underpaid, or delayed. At this point, policyholders should always consult, if not hire, an attorney. This may be a good time to bring in a public adjuster as well. While every claim is different, and I cannot possibly tell every policyholder whom to bring onto their team in this small chapter, we will discuss some of the most important team members and when to consider bringing them on board.

Policyholders should focus efforts on building the right professional team. You don't have to be the coach. You don't have to be the quarterback. You don't even have to play the game. But you do have to assemble the right team.

Doing so requires a bit of know-how, which is why I am writing this book. I want to empower policyholders to find the right experts and professionals to help them get their claims paid in full in a timely manner. That means knowing whom to bring on your team and when.

The following nine-step guide will walk you through the property insurance claims process with that role in mind. These steps are listed chronologically, especially the first few, but certain triggering events can result in skipping ahead to the end. These are general guidelines, but property insurance claims are far too varied and complex for this outline to be exhaustive or absolute. When in doubt, refer to your team for guidance.

STEP ONE: MAKE SURE EVERYONE IS SAFE.

Immediately following a loss, make sure everyone is safe. The same dangers that threaten property also threaten lives. Floods, fires, high winds, molds and toxins, intruders, and other dangers can lead to loss of life or health just as easily as loss of property. Make sure everyone is safe before doing anything else, and do not inspect a damaged and unsafe structure full of toxic debris.

STEP TWO: KEEP A RUNNING CHRONOLOGY.

Keep a written record of everything that happens. Keeping a running chronology of what you do, whom you speak to, what they say and do, and what you observe to be important. List everything and keep all receipts, invoices, business cards, and anything having to do with the claim. The claims process can be a blur, and keeping a complete chronology of events as they happen can help tremendously.

> **The claims process can be a blur, and keeping a complete chronology of events as they happen can help tremendously.**

STEP THREE: MITIGATE AGAINST FURTHER DAMAGE.

Property insurance policies generally require policyholders to take steps to mitigate and prevent further damage after a loss. Board up or put plastic over broken windows. Turn off the water if you might have busted pipes. Secure the area so that trespassers don't come onto the premises. Patch roofs, temporarily if need be, to avoid water and mold damage. Do whatever you can to prevent a loss from leading to bigger losses.

The cost of mitigation efforts is usually covered under the policy, as it saves the insurance company money. Failure to mitigate further damage could result in those subsequent losses being ineligible for coverage. Once everyone is safe, do what you can to mitigate against further damage, and document the steps taken.

Do not put your life or health or others' lives or health at risk. You should never enter an unsafe structure or return to the site of a loss until any possible dangers are removed. Don't go rushing into a smoldering building. Don't dig through toxic rubble or go wading through dangerous floodwaters. Don't expose yourself or others to toxins just to prevent loss of property. Hire skilled workers to carry out these mitigation efforts, which are often dangerous.

STEP FOUR: REPORT THE INSURANCE CLAIM.

Once everyone is safe and you have taken steps to mitigate against further damage, alert the insurance company to the loss. At this time, you should also touch base with your insurance agent or broker. Explain the situation and ask for advice.

For large losses, this is a good time to consult your attorney as well. For commercial clients with large losses, this can mean looping in in-house attorneys or putting a lawyer on retainer. For individual losses, this can be as simple as getting a free or low-cost consultation with a property insurance lawyer.

STEP FIVE: READ YOUR POLICY.

> **As a layperson, you will not understand everything— that's okay. Read it anyway.**

People don't read policies before buying them. Most insurance companies won't give you a copy of the policy until you buy it. People often don't even read policies *after* buying them. They probably should, but they generally don't. That's just human nature. But please, at least do yourself a favor after a loss and read your policy from start to finish. Every single word or clause is there for a reason. As a layperson, you will not understand everything—that's okay. Read it anyway, and try to understand as much as possible.

Look for a section labeled something to the effect of "Conditions After Loss" or "Duties in the Event of a Loss." This section will list the policyholder's obligations. Every policy is a little different, so be sure to understand what steps you are required to complete after a loss occurs. There are many obligations that must be executed immediately or within a short time frame. You may have to hire others to do them for you.

In addition to the provisions providing coverage and benefits, you must also pay attention to exclusions. Sections on provisions and exclusions can help you understand what is and is not covered under your policy. Policyholders are often surprised by the exclusions.

Make note of critical deadlines. Many policies require certain steps to be taken within a certain time frame. Typically, you must give notice of the claim right away. Next, most policies require policyholders to submit proof of loss within a certain time frame, often within sixty days. Some large or complex losses might take longer than the allotted time to fully assess and document. Many policies also require lawsuits over disputes to be filed within a year.

Do not let these deadlines pass. Seek legal counsel as soon as possible if you don't think you can meet a deadline. Claims attorneys may be able to get you an extension, but these actions take time. You don't want to be reaching out to an attorney when a critical deadline is near. I want to stress here that the most prudent action is to get professional help from those who have done this before, and contact an attorney immediately if you think you will miss a deadline, your claim is being delayed, or significant amounts owed are not quickly forthcoming.

STEP SIX: CONSIDER HIRING A PUBLIC ADJUSTER.

Public adjusters can guide you through the claims process. Not every policyholder needs to hire a public adjuster. With smaller claims, your agent or broker can fill this role, but sometimes it makes sense to hire a claims expert.

In addition to offering guidance, public adjusters can meet many of your obligations under the policy for you. They can file forms, compile proof and documentation of loss, and fulfill many of the other obligations listed under the "Conditions After Loss" section of your policy. These obligations must be met promptly. Many busy people will simply not have the time to do this themselves. Hiring a public adjuster puts an expert on your team who can do these tasks for you and make sure that all paperwork is filed accurately and in a timely manner. Most important, public adjusters help measure what you are owed under the policy following a property loss.

Someone must stay on top of the claims process. If you don't have the time, hire a public adjuster who does. Otherwise you could lose your rights and benefits.

STEP SEVEN: CONSIDER CONTACTING AN ATTORNEY.

Whether you need an attorney depends on the nature and size of your claim. You want to get an attorney in the event of a denied, partially denied, or significantly delayed claim. However, even in the absence of a dispute, speaking with an insurance claims attorney may still be prudent and provide valuable expertise. Property insurance attorneys can do more than just represent you in court. They can inform you when *you* should be disputing the insurance company's estimates, time frame, or processes.

Business policyholders dealing with large or complex losses should probably seek legal consultation immediately just for advice. Even smaller claims on individual policies may be worth picking up the phone to discuss with a lawyer if you have questions or concerns. Many attorneys offer low-cost consultations. They will offer initial advice and guidance. With smaller claims, your agent or broker can fill this role, but there's no harm in consulting an attorney.

The fee for these initial services should be small. You should not be paying a large contingency fee or percentage at this stage of a property insurance claim, nor should you lock yourself into a large contract with an attorney. Businesses with large losses might want to consider putting an attorney on retainer if they don't have sufficient in-house counsel, but the average policyholder can simply go in for a quick consultation.

STEP EIGHT: ASSESS YOUR SITUATION AND ASSEMBLE YOUR TEAM.

By this time, you should have spoken with your agent or broker and perhaps an attorney or public adjuster as well. Hopefully everything is going well, the insurance company is helpful and communicative, and your claim is moving forward toward payment and resolution.

Sometimes the insurance company will offer to handle everything for you. Sometimes they do a great job. But having seen how problems arise during the claims process, I advise skepticism. You cannot always trust the insurance industry's experts and adjusters to get things right. You cannot even be sure they are *trying* for accuracy. They work for the insurance company and its claims department. Their primary goals, at least within many insurance companies, is to "keep control" of the claim and pay less in benefits.

Do not be passive in the claims process, especially if you are dealing with a large loss. Now is the time to assess your situation and shore up your team. Commercial clients with large losses need larger teams to stay on top of the claims process as it moves forward.

That team should include the experts and professionals you have spoken with already. Your team can include your agent or broker, any legal counsel, public adjusters, contractors, accountants, architects, engineers, and other people involved with the claims process and valuing the amount of damage.

Depending on the nature of the loss, you may need to hire your own engineers, estimators, and other experts to make sure that the insurance company's estimates are accurate and that repairs are being done properly. Again, the size and makeup of your team is highly dependent upon the nature of your loss and the claim. The most important thing is getting the right people in place to provide the guidance and support you need to navigate the claims process. They should all work together to make sure that your claim is paid in full and repairs and restorations are done properly. Staying on top of the claims process often helps keep you out of litigation. That is why you need all these people. Going it alone, as tempting as it may be to cut costs, is a case of being penny-wise and pound-foolish. The right team not only helps you resolve a dispute that may arise but also helps avoid one.

> **Going it alone, as tempting as it may be to cut costs, is a case of being penny-wise and pound-foolish.**

STEP NINE: IF YOUR CLAIM GOES UNPAID, SUBSTANTIALLY UNDERPAID, OR SIGNIFICANTLY DELAYED— IT'S ALWAYS TIME TO GET LEGAL ADVICE ABOUT YOUR OPTIONS.

Unfortunately disputes are sometimes unavoidable. Talking to an insurance claims attorney early for advice is prudent. Hiring a knowledgeable and experienced insurance claims attorney once there is a problem is mandatory. You need someone to represent you—and not just in court. Claims attorneys can keep you out of court. They can represent you in talks with the insurance company and sometimes resolve the dispute without litigation, arbitration, or appraisal.

If your agent or broker cannot resolve a dispute, it is time to get an attorney. There are things that an attorney can do that an agent or broker cannot. There are also steps attorneys can take that even public adjusters cannot. The more serious the dispute, the more you need a good attorney to champion your case.

Do not be afraid to get an attorney. Too many people avoid seeking legal representation until it's too late. They think it is too much hassle or too expensive. The idea of calling a lawyer induces anxiety. People mostly call attorneys when something bad happens—be it a death, an arrest, a divorce, or some other significant loss. Sometimes people simply walk away from a legitimate claim rather than deal with the hassle. They may know they are being underpaid—though not always *how much* they are being underpaid—but simply choose not to dispute the insurance company's decision. They don't want to "waste" money on legal fees. They don't like dealing with lawyers.

Not consulting an attorney when

When you walk away, the insurance company wins.

your claim isn't paid in full is generally a mistake. No one likes experiencing a loss. No one wants to fight over a claim. No one likes having to retain counsel. But ignoring the situation only makes it worse. When you walk away, the insurance company wins. When you don't get proper representation, you may well forfeit rights and benefits you didn't know you even had.

Disputing a case *isn't* always worth the risk or expense. Sometimes legal costs can make a legitimate claim not worth pursuing, especially smaller claims. But a good lawyer will be up front about the costs and risks. They'll let you know whether you have a case. You might not—but you also might. You might be entitled to benefits you aren't getting. You don't know what you don't know.

If you have read this far into this book, you know the many stories we have of helping people collect millions more than they thought they were owed. Here is one more.

After Hurricane Andrew blew through southern Florida in 1992, a regional grocery chain, Farm Stores, suffered severe damage at several of their Miami locations. They called us because they were unhappy with what the insurance company was paying. They believed they were owed more. They didn't know the half of it. When we went down to visit the affected stores, I saw that their unique signs were still down. Following the hurricane, the sign companies were overloaded with orders. Sign orders were backed up for months. Many businesses had no signs.

"I thought you said the stores were back up and running?" I asked.

"They are," one of the owners said.

"No, no. I mean back up and running *like before*," I said. "They should still be paying you for interruption to business."

The company was under the impression that coverage for business interruption ended when the stores reopened. But that's not always the case. Policies generally cover lost revenue until the stores have returned to *normal* operations. Without the signs back up, they hadn't returned to normal operations.

Farm Stores is known for its iconic sign. Each location has a large sign featuring a spotted cow. You can't miss them. The sign is part of the chain's identity. In southern Florida, the spotted cow signs are as iconic as McDonald's golden arches. When businesses don't have their signs up, the public assumes they aren't open for business. I was sure the missing signs were costing them revenue—and sure enough they were losing money, and the accounting department had the data to prove it.

This lost revenue had not been included as part of their claim. We filed the extra losses on the claim and gathered market research from a university professor showing the effect of downed storefront signs. We shared this information with the insurance company, and the matter was resolved quickly. Our clients recovered far more money than they expected.

Everyone was so overjoyed by the benefit money that our law firm agreed to donate $50,000 of our fee to the University of Miami. Now, I am a Florida Gator from the University of Florida, but I was happy to help the university raise money for development and to give back to the local community.

This case shows what you might lose when you don't know what you don't know. Not all cases go this way, of course. Sometimes the insurance company is right. Sometimes the fight isn't worth the small potential gains. But you won't know where you stand if you don't have the right attorney on your team with the relevant knowledge and know-how to assess the situation.

A good attorney can often help you avoid litigation entirely. In the case of Farm Stores, which we discussed earlier, they had a whole team involved. They had hired a public adjuster. The CFO and accounting department were heavily involved. They had their own contractors. What they didn't have was an outside claims attorney—until they hired me. Had they brought me on sooner, I would have been able to make the same case about the signs earlier in the process. We could quite possibly have avoided litigation altogether. That would have been a more ideal outcome, but by the time they brought me on, they were already locked in litigation.

HOW TO FIND A GOOD ATTORNEY

The *right* attorney is key. You want an attorney who has substantial experience getting insurance claims paid. Make sure they have worked in the relevant area of law. Disputes over property insurance claims are best fought by property insurance lawyers. Many attorneys are generalists and take on *some* property insurance claims without that being their focus. They could be great attorneys with lots of experience, but experience means little if it is the wrong experience. Someone who focuses on medical malpractice lawsuits is not the best lawyer for property insurance claims.

General litigators won't have a deep understanding of how insurance companies and claims departments work. They won't know the ins and outs of insurance policies. They won't have a deep understanding of the relevant case law. They won't have been around the block enough times to immediately spot when the insurance company is doing something wrong. In the case involving Farm Stores, I immediately recognized the missing signs as an undeclared portion of the claim because I had previously worked cases like this. General litigators simply don't have as much experience with property insurance claims. You want an attorney who focuses daily on getting insurance claims paid to the exclusion of almost everything else.

Working on insurance claims is not enough, especially for large or complex claims. Insurance law is broad. There are lawyers who focus on medical claims. There are those who focus on disability claims. Lawyers like me do property insurance to the exclusion of all else.

Your attorney should have hands-on experience working cases just like yours. There is no way to learn an area of law by only studying case law. Property insurance attorneys working homeowners insurance cases have to understand the restoration process. They have to know the correct materials and methods for roofing a house to tell if the insurance company is doing it right. You learn this by attending conferences, talking to contractors, and working actual cases.

Do not always trust advertisements for legal services. Television commercials and online ads make it very easy for anybody to market themselves as specialists in many areas.

Do not always trust advertisements for legal services. Television commercials and online ads make it very easy for anybody to market themselves as specialists in many areas. They'll wear one hat in one advertisement as an expert and another in the next. There are many general litigators marketing themselves as property insurance attorneys (and a slew of other things) even though they work across many areas of law.

As with hiring an agent or a public adjuster, look for an attorney with the right qualifications and credentials. They should be in good standing with the state bar. They should have good references. The best lawyers are leaders in their field and command the respect of their peers. Their passion for their field of law will show in their participation in professional organizations. The best lawyers publish articles and educate others on their area of the law.

Finally, consider the lawyer as a person. The attorney-client relationship is just that—a *relationship*. The best insurance claims attorneys are true advocates of policyholders. This will show in how they talk to you. Do they listen? Are they respectful? Do they communicate well with you on an individual level? This is someone you may work closely with for months, possibly years. They will quarterback your whole insurance team. They should be someone you trust to represent you.

AFTERWORD

WE HAVE COVERED lots of ground in this book. Policyholders have much to watch out for these days: an automated and impersonal claims process that treats policyholders like numbers on a spreadsheet, the race-to-the-bottom business model common across the insurance industry, and a toxic culture in many claims departments that puts more emphasis on cost cutting than upholding promises to fully paying consumers.

My hope is that this book has been helpful and educational. I hope you've learned many things that will save you headaches and heartaches in the future when purchasing insurance and when making a claim. But I cannot possibly cover the entirety of insurance law, or even just property insurance law, in this small book. If you want to learn more, you can find more information in my blog www.propertyinsurancecoveragelaw.com, which is updated regularly.

If you have questions about a legal matter related to insurance, I welcome inquiries at cmerlin@merlinlawgroup.com or by phone at 813-229-1000. We love hearing from the public.

OUR SERVICES

CHIP MERLIN IS the president of Merlin Law Group, a national firm exclusively representing all types of policyholders in their fight for justice from their own insurance companies. Since 1985, Chip has fought tirelessly against bad faith insurers abandoning their promises to loyal policyholders in their time of need. As a highly sought-after keynote speaker, Chip frequents educational seminars, leading talks on insurance industry trends, ways to overcome bad faith insurer actions, and how policyholders and other groups can avoid insurance catastrophe. As a contributing writer to multiple blog series on property insurance law, Chip provides direct insight into a wide range of insurance topics.

Chip is devoted to educating others on insurance law, and his lively discussions point out how your insurance should work *with* you, not against you.

Twitter: @Chip_Merlin

Facebook: facebook.com/ChipMerlin

LinkedIn: linkedin.com/in/chip-merlin-15aaa811

ABOUT THE AUTHOR

ATTORNEY CHIP MERLIN has grown the Merlin Law Group into one of the largest US firms representing policyholders in disputes against their own insurance companies. Advising CNN, Fox News, Fox Business News, and local television outlets around the country, he's been dubbed "the Babe Ruth of Hurricane Claims" and "the Master of Disaster" by the press.

Former chair for the Bad Faith Insurance Litigation Group for the American Association for Justice, Chip has been blogging about helping consumers with their claims for more than ten years. He wrote *Pay Up!* to help all people become better negotiators and advocates for themselves.

When not taking on big insurance companies, the former marathon runner can be found racing sailboats.